Images of Jesus

Alfred McBride, O. Praem.

IMAGES OF JESUS

Ten Invitations to Intimacy

St.
Anthony
Messenger
Press

CINCINNATI, OHIO

Nihil Obstat: Rev. Nicholas Lohkamp, O.F.M.
Rev. Edward J. Gratsch

Imprimi Potest: Rev. John Bok, O.F.M.
Provincial

Imprimatur: Rev. R. Daniel Conlon, Vicar General and Chancellor
Archdiocese of Cincinnati
July 1, 1993

The *nihil obstat* and *imprimatur* are a declaration that a book is considered to be free from doctrinal or moral error. It is not implied that those who have granted the *nihil obstat* and *imprimatur* agree with the contents, opinions or statements expressed.

The author is grateful for permission to use excerpts from the following works: Unless otherwise noted, Scripture citations are taken from *The New American Bible With Revised New Testament,* copyright ©1986 by the Confraternity of Christian Doctrine, and are used by permission. All rights reserved. Scripture texts taken from *The New Jerusalem Bible,* copyright ©1966 by Darton, Longman & Todd Ltd., and Doubleday, a division of Bantam Doubleday Dell Publishing Group, Inc., are used by permission of the publisher. The excerpt from Father Neil Heery's diary is used with his permission. The excerpt from *Three Philosophies of Life,* by Peter Kreeft, copyright ©1989 by Ignatius Press, is reprinted with permission of the publisher. The excerpt from *Heaven,* by Peter Kreeft, copyright ©1989 by Ignatius Press, is reprinted with the permission of the publisher. The excerpt from *People of the Lie* by M. Scott Peck, M.D., copyright ©1983 by M. Scott Peck, M.D., is reprinted with the permission of the publisher, Simon and Schuster. Excerpts (including quotations from St. Augustine's *Confessions*) from *Augustine of Hippo: A Biography,* by Peter Brown, copyright ©1967 by Peter Brown, are reprinted with permission of University of California Press. Prayer at the Preparation of the Altar and the Gifts is taken from the English Translation of the Roman Missal, copyright ©1973, International Comission on English in the Liturgy. All rights reserved. Quotations from St. Basil, St. Leo the Great, St. Bernard, an ancient Holy Saturday homily, an ancient Easter homily and the Easter antiphons are taken from *The Liturgy of the Hours,* copyright ©1973, International Commission on English in the Liturgy. All rights reserved. Quotations from John Henry Newman are taken from *Parochial and Plain Sermons,* copyright ©1987 by Ignatius Press and are reprinted with permission of the publisher. The excerpt from "The Quickening of John the Baptist," by Thomas Merton, in *The Collected Poems of Thomas Merton,* copyright ©1977 by Our Lady of Gethsemani Monastery, is reprinted by permission of New Directions Publishing Corp.

Cover and book design by Julie Lonneman
Cover photo by Gene Plaisted, O.S.C., of detail from icon by Felix and Emma Senger in Pax Christi Church, Eden Prairie, Minnesota

ISBN 0-86716-180-9

©1993, Alfred McBride, O. Praem.
All rights reserved.

Published by St. Anthony Messenger Press
Printed in the U.S.A.

Contents

INTRODUCTION

1

Chapter One

JESUS, MY FRIEND

Two Souls in One Body

7

Chapter Two

JESUS, MY HEALER

Four Powerful Remedies

31

Chapter Three

JESUS, MY TEACHER

The Master of Meditation

55

Chapter Four

JESUS, MY LORD

The Son of God

75

Chapter Five

JESUS, MY MENTOR

The Three Stages of Discipleship

97

Chapter Six

JESUS, MY SERVANT LEADER
The Social Gospel
119

Chapter Seven

JESUS, MY SAVIOR
Liberation From Sin
143

Chapter Eight

JESUS, MY EVANGELIZER
Spreading the Gospel
165

Chapter Nine

JESUS, MY CROSS-BEARER
Four Reasons for the Crucifixion
187

Chapter Ten

JESUS, MY JOY
Experiencing Easter
207

CONCLUSION
231

Introduction

Once upon a time there was an Irishman who lived in
a single room in Galway town. One night he dreamed
of a treasure tucked beneath a bridge in Dublin. The
dream returned the next two nights. Unable to
dismiss it from his mind, he traveled to Dublin to find
the money. He discovered the exact spot, but there
was no treasure there. Depressed, he talked about
this with a policeman. The officer laughed and said,
"Sure, you should pay no attention to dreams. Why,
the other night I dreamed about a box of money
hidden in the walls of a room of a house in Galway."
Unwittingly, the policeman described the very room
in which this man lived. The officer concluded, "Of
course, no sensible man would believe in dreams."

Our friend was amazed by the policeman's story.
He smiled, hastily said good-bye and rushed back
home. He raced to his room, opened a wall and found
a box of money that settled him for life. The treasure
had always been with him. To find it he had to make a
long journey. He needed direction to his goal from a
stranger.

Jesus is the treasure hidden in the room inside
us, our spirit. To find him we must take a journey. Not

all over the earth, like Ulysses sailing the dangerous seas: Our journey is within. We do not have to go far, but we must dig deep.

This book is a guide for the trip. None of us walks alone. I have needed a guide for my journey. I share with you here some hints about your own search. There are many possible routes. I choose here ten images of Jesus.

An image is more than a snapshot. It is a revelation. During a recent trip to Russia I saw many icons. The figures were not exact replicas of what people look like. They were people transformed by grace and sanctity. They were revelations. I saw hundreds of people light candles before these icons and then bow deeply before them. They were not worshiping idols; they were acknowledging disclosures of holiness. They were in touch with the saints. They communed with the beyond in our midst.

Think of the images of Jesus in this book in much the same spirit. I have selected ten images of Jesus from the Gospels. Each one invites you to a relationship with him. Each Gospel image calls you to walk through the picture into a world where Jesus lives. The scriptural icon awakens you and me to a world within ourselves that we seldom notice because of daily cares. Our inner space is just as vast and mysterious as outer space. Our souls and spirits are vaster than oceans. When we have a peak experience of Jesus, it is not out of place to say it causes "oceanic dizziness."

Jesus said it all so simply. "The kingdom of God is among you" (Luke 17:21c). The treasure is inside us. Scripture loves to describe us as sleepers. We dream-walk through the outer world and fail to notice the excitement within.

> It is the hour now for you to awake from sleep. For our salvation is nearer now than when we first believed. (Romans 13:11b)

> Awake, O sleeper,
>   and arise from the dead,
> and Christ will give you light. (Ephesians 5:13b)

What is this scriptural sleep? It is our inadvertence to our inner space. We are wide awake to what is transient. We sleep and thus do not hear the music of the spheres within. We are awake to the latest news, which is usually full of the folly of life. We sleep through the news that is always good. We build our outer lives on sand. We could fashion them from the rock that waits within.

Our inner world is not a simple and easy world to explore, but it is definitely worth the effort. More than anyone, St. Augustine was aware of its sheer size. With his usual cold-water realism, in his *Confessions*, Augustine frankly spoke of the challenge of an inner journey that seemed to him like a trek through a limitless forest.

> This memory of mine is a great force, a vertiginous mystery, my God, a hidden depth of infinite complexity: and this is my soul, and this is what I am. What then, am I, my God? What then is my true nature? A living thing, taking innumerable forms, quite limitless.... Command what you wish, but give what you command.

If we did not have a faith that tells us that Jesus and his Holy Spirit lovingly await within, we might fear the journey. We need not. Whenever heaven touches earth, the first words are "Do not be afraid." Jesus comes to us with the love that casts out fear. The Holy Spirit is a presence of peace in which there is no fear. Jesus tells us to yearn for God as a thirsty person longs for water. What he tells us is what our spirit already knows, for our spirit is the locus of absolute longing that settles for nothing less than absolute fulfillment.

Our bodies go about the business of earth. Our souls—our minds and wills—when on their best behavior, play with the business of human knowledge and the worthwhile projects of this world. But our spirits—our deepest selves—are only at home with eternity. Again, Augustine: "Behold, sometimes, we are made glad by a certain inner sweetness. Yes, our mind has been able to catch a glimpse, for a fleeting instant, of something above change.... Now I have a sense throughout my being of something beyond time."

The ten images of Jesus in this book are wake-up calls for our spirits. The images complement each other, woven together more like a tapestry than like ten discrete pictures in a gallery. Jesus is one. He cannot be cut apart and looked at like a limb in a scanner.

I should say what this book is not. Look in vain for an abstract Christology. That is not my competence. Search fruitlessly for abstract traits of Jesus to be used as role models for our attitudes. That may happen only incidentally. Forage in frustration for analyses of great art depictions of Jesus. This is not art history; it is a modest attempt at spirituality.

Each expository chapter is followed by a series of spiritual exercises for meditation, self-examination, shared prayer or some other form of spiritual self-discovery. At times you will see my Irish melancholy overtake the material. I like to blame Augustine or Newman for that, but I take full responsibility for it myself. I trust that more obvious will be the joy of Christ and his Good News for us.

I am grateful for the motivation to do this book from the staff of St. Anthony Messenger Press, especially Carol Luebering. I also thank the following priests who helped me shape the outline and clear up some difficulties I encountered along the way: Francis Kelly, John Farley, William Seifert and Philip Wilson.

Chapter One

JESUS, MY FRIEND

Two Souls in One Body

The deepest longing you will ever have is the ability
to make a friend—ultimately, to be a friend of God.
Your most persistent hunger is for a satisfying
companion. You may want to be rich, powerful and
attractive, but unless you become someone's friend,
your other desires will disappoint you. As Aristotle
said, "Without friends no one would choose to live,
though he had all other goods. Friendship is one soul
living in two bodies."

The awesome ninth symphony of Beethoven
crests with an ecstasy of choral and instrumental
sound, celebrating the joy that comes from
friendship. Beethoven places his magnificent music at
the service of Schiller's poetry:

> Whoever has created
> An abiding friendship,
> ...All who can call but one soul theirs
> Join in our song of praise.

The experience of one deep friendship causes us to
look with a benign heart on the whole world.

> You millions, I embrace you!

This kiss is for all the world!

Of all the gifts we can receive from Jesus, the capacity to be a friend is the greatest. He knows how to be a friend. In Galilee and Judea Jesus tried to be a friend to all kinds of people. Today he seeks to be your friend and mine. "I no longer call you slaves,... I have called you friends..." (John 15:15a, c).

If you want to be a friend, you will find the secret in Christ's way of doing it. If you are lonely, unappreciated and unwanted, you can discover in him a path to community and friendship. The story of how he offered friendship to others is found in the New Testament. The saints of Church history have shared with us their personal experiences of Christ's friendliness. People in our families, parishes and workplaces continue to tell us of Christ's affectionate approach to them.

Jesus shows us how to become a friend. He has the ability to save a heart from breaking. He can ease the ache of life and cool its pain. He does this by his example in the Gospels and by his friendly presence to us today.

I cannot enumerate all the ways he does this, but the following ones seem to be the most effective. I admit in advance that each of us is unique, with a singular personality, a particular family background, an ethnic heritage and a social history that is ours alone. I also believe that Christ's wise counsel about friendship is adaptable to every human being. Here are his friendship principles.

Think Like a Friend

Friendship in the mind produces friendship in life. To think like a friend is to show interest in people. Jesus demonstrated a lively interest in all kinds of people from a rich playboy to a poor widow. He was interested in the safety of an adulteress about to be stoned and the medical needs of a traveler beaten and robbed by muggers.

He liked hearing the opinions and thoughts of others. "What say you? What think you? What do people think of me?" He could reflect on a seed or on the stone mass of the Temple and find a message for others in them. No detail about people escaped him. He noticed the prominent tassels on the sashes of the Pharisees and a hemorrhaging woman's hopeful tug on the hem of his own robe even though a crowd was shoving against him.

His lively interest in others was the secret of their interest in him. The more he thought about their needs, the more people awoke to a fascination with him. He thought like a friend. Others sensed this and were attracted to him. Jesus was interested enough in you and me to come and live with us, first in Galilee and Jerusalem and today in our hearts. His concern for us initiates our friendship with him and reveals how we can be friends with others.

When St. Augustine wrote the story of his conversion, he cited the prayers of his mother, the sermons of Ambrose and the shortcomings of his intellectual pursuits as elements of his journey to faith. What moved him most was the impassioned interest Jesus showed in him. He wrote of a Jesus who tried every available means to let him know how much he was loved:

> You called, you shouted and you broke through my deafness. You flashed, you shone, and you dispelled my blindness. You breathed your fragrance on me. I drew in breath and now I pant for you. I have tasted you. Now I hunger and thirst for more. You touched me and I burned for your peace.

Many of us live too much inside the range of our own interests. We make ourselves the sun and expect people to be like planets circling around us. So long as we assume that our concerns are the most important in the world and everyone else's troubles are secondary, we will have difficulty in becoming a friend. Jesus strongly recommends a change in that perspective: Begin to show interest in others. Acts of genuine interest in other people will result in their desire to be closer to us. A friendly mind makes a friendly life.

Like most people, I am occasionally at a social gathering. When I lend an attentive ear to someone who wants to talk, I invariably discover that the person relaxes, shares and enjoys the encounter. Even if I have hardly said a word for as much as an hour, my companion will often remark, "You are certainly an interesting person."

Everyone likes to be noticed, valued and heard. Our interest in them is not for commercial or manipulative reasons. Our goal is spiritual. Our attentiveness is practice in becoming a friend. We give others the pleasure of discovering their own importance. The more we touch others personally, the more they will be open to an inner meeting with

Jesus and the gifts he will bring them.

Behave Like a Friend

A friend in need is a friend indeed. To behave like a friend is to do a good turn for others. In the Twelve Step program for people recovering from various addictions, the members are advised to perform at least one good deed each day for someone—and not get found out.

Jesus behaved like a friend. Often, after he had cured someone, he added, "Don't tell anyone." He was happy and content with the joy he had caused in others. He did not require praise for his good works. His pleasure was in the giving.

He dined as a family friend at the home of Martha and Mary and cured the fever of Peter's mother-in-law. He performed numerous acts of friendship for perfect strangers: raising the son of a widow in Naim, curing a blind beggar, healing the servant of a Roman soldier, performing dozens of miracles for the nameless crowds that surged toward him. His friendly ways drew people to him then and attracts us to him today. He helps us to behave like a friend.

The best way to become a friend is to act like one. Give others the inexpressible comfort of feeling safe with you. Help them to talk without worrying that you will censor their words. Take what is worth keeping and with kindness forget the rest. I have found that the more attention I pay to others' needs, the more my capacity for friendship grows. Every act of friendly behavior enlarges our hearts. This means losing self-absorption to gain a richer prize, the art of friendship.

One of the most beloved filmmakers was Frank Capra. Every Christmas we cry and laugh again at his *It's a Wonderful Life*. Early on, he realized that he should stop making films for actors and start making them for audiences. "The art of Frank Capra is very, very simple," he said in 1982, when he won the American Film Institute's Life Achievement Award. "It's the love of people. And add two simple ideals to this love of people—the freedom of each individual and the equal importance of each individual."

His point pertains here. What he says about the art of a successful film is just as true of the art of friendship: behaving in a loving way toward people.

The saints knew how to behave like friends. They were not so taken with heavenly affairs that they did not work on their friendships. Famed, saintly friendships come to mind immediately: Vincent de Paul and Louise de Marrilac, John of the Cross and Teresa of Avila, Francis de Sales and Jane de Chantal. Their friendships energized their growth in faith and motivated them to enthusiastic loving care for the sick, the poor, the needy, the lonely and those who hunger for spiritual growth.

Come back a moment with me to the fourth century to the story of Basil and Gregory. In Cappadocia (modern eastern Turkey), they ministered as bishops. They were lifelong friends. Basil described their friendship in this manner:

> ...[W]e began to feel affection for each other. When, in the course of time, we acknowledged our friendship and recognized that our ambition was a

life of true wisdom, we became everything to each
other: we shared the same lodging, the same table,
the same desires, the same goal. Our love for each
other grew daily warmer and deeper.... We seemed
to be two bodies with a single spirit.... [T]he great
name we wanted was to be Christians, to be called
Christians. (*Liturgy of the Hours*)

I like the simplicity of this description of friendship.
Basil and Gregory achieved what we all look for, the
ability to become a friend. What better goal does a
Christian have?

Feel Like a Friend

Sensitivity to the feelings of others is a necessary
component of friendship. Jesus wept with Martha and
Mary at the grave of their brother. He looked with
affection at the rich young man who was searching for
something better in life. He was moved with sorrow
and pity for people's troubles. He knew the roar of
anger and outbursts of joy. His ability to express his
feelings endeared many to him. He was not a cold
man. The Son of God was a warm human being.

I admit that the descriptions of Christ's feelings
are not elaborated in the Gospels. Those spare texts
record just hints of Christ's capacity for feeling: a
sigh, a groan, a tear, a shout of anguish, a look of
tenderness. St. Augustine faced this reality in his
commentaries on the Gospels. Given to lyrical
expressions of emotions himself, he searched for a
legitimate method to speak of Christ's feelings. He
found his answer in the teaching on the Mystical

Body of Christ. To him the unity of the body was in the soul, where the emotions were experienced. Since we are members of Christ's Body, we have access to his inner life—especially when we pray the Psalms. As Peter Brown writes in *Augustine of Hippo*,

> Seen in this light, the Psalms were the record of the emotions of Christ and his members. Just as he had taken on human flesh, so Christ had, of his own free will, opened himself to human feeling. These feelings are only hinted at in the Gospels. Often, the Christ of Augustine's sermons is the pale impassive figure of a Late Roman mosaic. His crucifixion is a solemn measured act, the sleep of a lion. But when he turns to the Psalms, Augustine will draw from them the immensely rich deposit of human emotions. For here was Christ speaking directly in the passionate King David.

Because Jesus could—and did—express sympathy, empathy and compassion for people, he moved them. In the same way, he touches us and shows us our capacity for empathy. His overtures of friendship are more than an idea in the head and a good deed done, essential as those are. He touches our hearts because he allows himself to be touched by us today. He feels for us as a friend does.

Jesus calls you and me to show our feelings of friendship for others. This means we must allow ourselves to be affected by the lives of those we meet. If they cry, we cry. If they laugh, we laugh. If they show anger, so can we. One reason why so much is written today about cultivating and expressing emotions is that there has been too much repression of those gifts from God. So we are advised to hug people, to be comfortable with our feelings, to be sensitive to the feelings of others, to take a "feelings check."

I realize that feelings are not a substitute for rational judgment, that emotions can swing out of control and that unguided sexual feelings can lead to wrong behavior. It is a question of balance. Human beings feel. Denial of feeling is dishonesty with self. We must strive for inner harmony that includes the exercise of reason, the expression of feeling and the will to good behavior. We will grow in friendship when we are willing to touch others and let them affect our emotional life. Our heart is the bridge to the hearts around us.

Become a Best Friend

The apostle John was known as the disciple Jesus loved. In other words, he was Christ's best friend. He belonged to the inner circle of Christ's companions. Jesus favored him more than Peter, James or Andrew; John was the intimate, private friend. At the Last Supper he reclined in the honored position next to Jesus and rested his head upon Christ's heart. The other apostles were bridges between the crowds and Jesus. John was the apostles' line of communication with Jesus. From the cross, Jesus entrusted his mother to John.

Is it possible that the Son of God would have a best friend? Surely the Son of the Most High is not supposed to love one person more than another! We expect Jesus to have loved everyone with equal affection or, at least, we conclude that he would have loved people with the same devotion they displayed toward him. The truth is that Jesus was entirely human in his feelings. There is nothing contrary to the gospel spirit in this. Christian love is consistent with having a best friend.

What shall we say to those who argue that Christian love should embrace every human being equally? Theoretically, our goal is to meet every person with goodwill and kindness. Practically, we must begin with a few people. The best preparation for friendship to all is to act in a friendly manner to those who are near us. We begin with those we know and enlarge our affection for those we do not know. If we start by loving the world first we will be like the cynics who say that they love humanity but cannot stand people.

Love is a habit that demands practice. We cannot practice on the whole human race. We are able to work on our relationships with those who are close to us. Building a deep friendship takes a lot of time and patience. We learn how to accede to another's wishes even when they are contrary to our own. We concentrate on a friend's good points and try to imitate them. Over many days, months and years we quietly root love and cultivate affection in our hearts. This is the process of becoming a best friend to one person and a very close friend to a few more. This is the school of friendship that trains us to be sensitive to the needs of strangers, acquaintances, coworkers and, ultimately, the whole human family.

Focus on Others' Virtues

Jesus understood that we will not *like* everyone we meet. Some people will irritate us. Personality conflicts are bound to happen. Cultural differences will cause misunderstandings. The possibility of friendship collapses because we do not like the way some people dress, their choice of colors, their taste in music, the pitch of their voices, their political commitment, facial tics or raucous laughter. They talk too much, ignore our brilliant insights, interrupt our explanations, finish our sentences for us and churlishly contradict whatever we say. They bring out the worst in us. Sometimes their irritating behavior is simply due to misunderstandings of a minor nature. How could we ever be friends with them?

In such cases Jesus advises us to use this disruptive experience for self-examination. Instead of concentrating on the insufferable behavior of others, we should treat the occurrence as an invitation to look at our own attitudes. "Stop judging that you may not be judged.... Why do you notice the splinter in your brother's eye, but do not perceive the wooden beam in your own eye? ...[R]emove the wooden beam from your eye first; then you will see clearly to remove the splinter from your brother's eye" (Matthew 7:1, 3, 5). That is Christ's first point for dealing with what we do not like in others.

Jesus also counsels us to focus on the positive values in each person. He knew that his listeners could not stand Samaritans. So he told the story of a Good Samaritan who was better at being a friendly neighbor than they were. They could not imagine a valid religious sentiment in a pagan soldier. Jubilantly, Jesus praised the faith of the Roman centurion who humbly protested that his home was not worthy of Jesus. They could see no redeeming qualities in any hated tax collector. Yet Jesus pointed out the potential of one tax collector, Matthew, to become a close friend in Jesus' community of apostles and revealed the generosity of another, Zacchaeus. They argued that sinners were beneath contempt. Jesus never approved of sin, but he willingly ate with sinners. He saw inside them the hunger for salvation; he ministered to them at the table of friendship.

Jesus insisted that we should look into our own hearts when faced with the faults of others—and then root out the greater faults in our own souls. After this, we should look outward and make an inventory of the positive virtues in those who bother us. First dispose of the vinegar of judgmentalism, then obtain the honey of insight into the attractive qualities of others. Christ's inward-outward strategy is obviously more difficult than it seems. The simplicity of his principles does not obscure their challenging application.

St. Therese of Lisieux wrote that one of the most infuriating aspects of convent life was the multitude of annoyances she experienced from other sisters. One of them fidgeted noisily with her rosary; another splashed soapy water in her face. A humorless one kept telling unfunny jokes, and so on. Small matters indeed, but magnified in a close environment.

Therese looked inward and concluded that the greater fault was her own immaturity and lack of tolerance, her unwillingness to take a deeper step in love and understanding. She also looked outward, challenging herself to perform a special act of kindness to any sister who annoyed her and to pray for her. She began to see in her difficult sisters attractive qualities she had missed before. So successful was she at this that the sister who actually irritated Therese the most thanked her for being such a warm friend.

Our goal of becoming a friend will require this inward-outward plan. If the faults of others drive us crazy, we should look inside, figure out our own faults and get rid of them. We are not asked to be dishonest and pretend the other has no faults. Rather, we are to acknowledge the reality of the nuisance and recognize an opportunity for growth. The second step is equally important: to pray for those who bother us and make a list of their appealing traits. The result will be a more forgiving attitude and, in many cases, the birth of an unexpected friendship.

The best in other people flows out to us when the best in us flows out to them. This is a slow process; we should not expect instant improvement. The soul, like a seed buried in the earth, grows surely, quietly, mysteriously and slowly.

Discover the Spiritual Purpose of Friendship

In John's account of the Last Supper, Jesus tells the apostles he is giving them a new commandment: "Love one another, as I love you.... You are my friends if you do what I command you" (John 15:12b, 14). What is new about this commandment? The Old Testament already commanded love of neighbor "as yourself" (see Leviticus 19:18). Jesus gave a fresh interpretation to this scriptural principle, enriching it by asking us to love people *as he did*. Hence our quest to become a friend has two models—the love we have for ourselves and the love Jesus has for people.

What is there in Christ's love that may be absent from our own love? The first five points in this chapter illustrated how our approach to friendship is quite similar to that of Jesus. With him we can think, behave and feel like a friend. Just like Christ we can focus on the virtues in others and have a best friend. What may be missing is our intention to help our friends discover God in their lives, to be a partner in their faith-journey, to witness to them the impact of Christ's salvation on our lives.

Whenever Jesus made a friend, he did everything he could to awaken in that person an awareness of God. When he walked with the two depressed people on the road to Emmaus, he went beyond relieving them of their distress. He opened them to the appealing presence of God. They said afterward that their hearts burned within them during their intimate encounter with Jesus. During his lengthy conversation with a Samaritan woman he met at a well, he led her to meet God and to accept salvation. She began by meeting a friendly man and ended by accepting a savior.

Our Christian friendships, therefore, should enable us to get in touch with the divine presence. Christian friendship is a faith partnership in which, by mutual witness, we make possible one another's growth in kingdom living and salvation behavior. We do this through example, prayer and dialogue.

Through Example

The evidence of our struggle to live by Christian moral standards, to be just and fair to all people, to be faithful to prayer and worship is a form of powerful personal witness to our friends. Our quest for God stirs up their own inner drive to seek God. Every act of devotion on our part is a silent stimulant to our close friends to look within themselves and consider their own journey to God.

Through Prayer

We pray for the needs and hopes of our friends, including praying forth—evoking in them—the power of the Spirit. We clearly want our friends to be physically and mentally healthy. In prayer we become acutely sensitive to their need for spiritual wholeness. Prayer stretches our inner vision of others so that we always have their spiritual interests at heart.

Through Dialogue

We find appropriate times to discuss spiritual and moral matters with those who are dear to us. There is a time and season for explicitly conferring about the spiritual matters that are essential to our Christian goals. St. Paul, who was skilled in all these forms of Christian friendship, spoke with extravagant warmth about the spiritual purpose of his friendship. "I long for all of you with the affection of Christ Jesus.... I long to depart this life and be with Christ.... [Yet] I shall remain and continue in the service of all of you for your progress and joy in the faith..." (Philippians 1:8b, 23b-25b).

When we practice this spiritual aspect of our friendship with those close to us, we will begin to act in the same way toward all in the ever-widening circle of people whom we will meet in the course of our lives.

Deepen Your Friendship With Jesus

If I speak of friendship with Jesus, am I talking about a relationship with a character in a book? Am I referring to a pleasant memory of a historical figure with whom I have a fantasy conversation? Am I summoning up a ghost, albeit unthreatening, upon whom I gaze with a dreamlike reverie? No, there is nothing basically unreal about my suggestion to work on a friendship with Jesus. I could not ask you to have a relationship with someone who is not actually there.

Jesus lives today. Jesus can be personally present to us today because he is the Son of God and has risen from the dead. The resurrection stories, which we will contemplate in the last chapter of this book, amply testify that Jesus is alive and present now. He wanted to be near us always and become our friend. "And look, I am with you always; yes, to the end of time" (Matthew 28:20b, *New Jerusalem Bible*).

This possibility is manifestly spiritual. That is not to say it is unreal. When we are in touch with our inner space and realize how alive we are there, we can begin to relate to Jesus as a friend. When we take an inner journey we become aware of this possibility.

The poet Yeats says that the journey to the inner self is not just an important one, but the only one. It will put us in touch with a silence beyond the noise of the outer world—and even of our inner racket. Then we are led to listen to the sound of Christ's presence beyond the silence.

Jesus wants to become our friend. "Behold, I stand at the door and knock. If anyone hears my voice and opens the door, [then] I will enter his house and dine with him, and he with me" (Revelation 3:20). The use of meal imagery demonstrates that Christ's intentions are friendly. He comes to have joyous communion with us.

How do we deepen our friendship with Jesus? By experiencing his presence in word, sacrament and service.

In Word

Love of Scripture, especially the Gospels, is an excellent path to becoming aware of the personal presence of Jesus. This will happen when we approach the text as divine revelation to which we react in faith. We may certainly consider its stories, poetry and wisdom sayings as literature. We should indeed benefit from historical and archaeological studies that unravel the complexities of Scripture. But only when we pray the Psalms, sing the canticles and contemplate the texts with faith will we begin to sense the spiritual presence of Jesus in our encounter with the Bible. Read with faith, the words of God reveal the Word of God.

A medieval ritual, "the sweetness of Scripture,"

grew out of this insight. To introduce a young person to the wonder of the Bible, a parchment page of Scripture was partly coated with a dab of honey. The sweetened page was formally presented to the youth for tasting, while a troubadour sang, "Taste and see how good the LORD is..." (Psalm 34:9a).

Then the child's father spoke of Elizabeth's compliment to Mary. "Blessed are you who believed..." (Luke 1:45). He taught his child that faith draws spiritual sweetness from the text. Just as Mary believed and then received Jesus, so our faith opens us to him.

Next, the child's mother would tell the story of the finding in the temple. When she came to the verse, "his mother kept all these things in her heart," (Luke 2:51b), she would instruct her youngster that the Scripture must be treasured in a prayerful heart, after the example of Mary.

Faith and contemplative attitude are basic for reading the Scriptures; they fill us with religious wonder. This is how we become friendlier with Jesus through the word of God.

In Sacrament

When we celebrate a sacrament we meet Jesus. This is especially true in the Eucharist, "in which is contained the whole spiritual good of the Church, namely, Christ himself..." (*Decree on the Ministry and Life of Priests*, #5). Jesus identified himself as the Bread of Life (see John 6:35). When we commune with Jesus in the Eucharist we experience him in the mystery of his saving death and resurrection. The profound simplicity of that encounter is something like gazing at the facets of a brilliant diamond. We behold Jesus through the gem-like light of Advent, Christmas, Epiphany, Lent, Easter and Pentecost—as well as in the festivals of the Blessed Mother, the martyrs, virgins, confessors and all the other saints.

The communal aspect of our celebration makes our personal relating to Jesus warmer because we benefit from the faith energy of the group. The Christian assembly also enables us to experience Jesus in his Mystical Body, the circle of friendship which is our Church.

The quality of our friendship with Jesus develops partly in connection with our stage of life—childhood, adolescence, young adulthood, middle age and sunset years. Age alone, however, does not determine the full intensity of our friendship with him. As a child, Catherine of Siena had already entered into a relationship with Jesus that surpassed what most of us experience after a lifetime of development. We are dealing here with the world of faith and mystery, which is not necessarily constrained by the variables of time.

Meeting Jesus in the Eucharist is enhanced by our ability to rest in meditation before his presence in the tabernacle. We will consider meditation at greater length later. When meditation is related to the Bread of Life, it becomes more than a relaxation exercise. It becomes a time of friendship with Jesus.

In Service

Most of our waking hours are spent in dealing with people. Jesus teaches that he comes to us in every person we encounter. He appears before us clothed in the needs of that person. He looks at us with that person's hunger for recognition, respect, affection, affirmation and love. His appeal is meant to help us see the inner thirsts of others and their outer needs as well. That is why he tells us that he will arrive at our door in the stranger, the homeless, the sick, the prisoner, the hurting and the hungry.

He is not asking us to be actors or to play fantasy games in order to imagine he is there. This is not a ruse to trick us into loving behavior. He is inviting us to faith in his presence in the poor, the ugly, the people everyone else loves to despise. On a less dramatic and somewhat easier level, he urges us to have faith in his presence in those whom we enjoy being with. We serve Jesus in others no matter how they come to us.

If our Christian service is to be a long-term commitment, we will need the perspective of faith in order to stay with it. This is not a sentimental journey or a life for romantic idealists. Every growing friendship demands discipline and hard work. Religious faith is the energizing factor. Finding friendship with Jesus through dedicated service is enormously satisfying—and sometimes infuriatingly hard. With loving faith, the burden is light and the yoke is easy.

Conclusion

These are seven ways in which Jesus becomes my friend and enables me to become friends with others. Permit me to summarize them here:

1) Think like a friend.

2) Behave like a friend.

3) Feel like a friend.

4) Become a best friend.

5) Focus on the other's virtues.

6) Discover the spiritual purpose of friendship.

7) Deepen your friendship with Jesus.

These paths are available to all people who approach friendship from the viewpoint of faith. They are not the only ways. Wise people have discovered numerous roads to friendship based on faith in Jesus. Yet I am certain that these seven steps are practical and immensely adaptable to a wide variety of human temperaments and situations. These are friendship starters which will be very helpful to all who pursue them with imagination, persistence, discipline, hope, generosity and a disposition to kindness.

Reflection

When Jesus becomes my friend, then I learn from the Master how to be a friend to others. Here are three exercises for getting closer to Jesus.

1) The Look of Love

Find a quiet and restful place. Assume a comfortable position and settle your body and your inner thoughts. Close your eyes and visualize one of your friends. Love that friend from your heart.

Now turn your attention to Jesus. See him hugging children and blessing them. Or pick another scene from the Gospels that appeals to you. Focus your interior gaze on Jesus. Love him in the same way—from your heart.

Each time you look at him and think of him with love, you will become more intimate with him and your capacity for friendship will grow. Do this at least twice a day, preferably early in the morning and just before retiring.

2) Word and Silence

At the beginning of each week select a phrase or a sentence from the prayers, psalms or readings of the Sunday liturgy. Choose a text that touches you. Adapt the words to your own situation. For example, "Jesus, your love never fails" or "To you I lift up my eyes" or "Jesus, I put my hope in you."

Make the line a recurring thought throughout

each day of the week. Write it out and put it where you can see it—on your pillow, on the refrigerator, on your desk. Say it slowly, one word at a time, letting silence intervene. Drop each word into the well of your consciousness. Let it sink into your inner life. Go from the word into silence. Each time you do this, you will move nearer to friendship with Jesus—and with others.

3) Recognizing Jesus

Think of someone who bothers you. Visualize that person. Say words of forgiveness for him or her. Remind yourself that Jesus comes to you in each one you meet. Look at the positive values in the one who annoys you. Everyone has good points; praise God for the gifts that person possesses. See the person who irritates you as bringing Jesus to you to ask you to enlarge your tolerance, forgiveness and love. Plan acts of generosity and kindness for the one you dislike. Be encouraged by the teaching of Jesus, "Whatever you do to others, you do to me" (see Matthew 25:40).

Prayer

Jesus, my friend,
I want to become friendlier to all those
  around me.
Teach me how to think, behave and feel like
  a friend.

Help me to focus on the virtues of others.
Develop in me the capacity to become a best
    friend to someone.
Show me the way to have a deeper
    relationship with you.
Walk with me and talk to me of love.
Make my heart an open house where all
    people can feel at home.

Chapter Two

JESUS, MY HEALER

Four Powerful Remedies

During Pope John Paul II's second pastoral visit to the United States, I served as one of the bishops' representatives to the media. My principal duty was to be available at the media center, usually a hotel ballroom large enough to accommodate three hundred reporters, to answer their questions about Catholic beliefs and practices or about a speech the pope had just given.

At each stop I was permitted to attend one of the day's events so that I would have a continuous concrete sense of what was happening. In Los Angeles I chose the pope's meeting with the leading powers of television and movies at the Sheraton Universal Hotel. Five hundred executives, producers, writers and media stars had gathered there.

Across the front of the room, TV monitors, suspended from the ceiling, showed the pope in a nearby auditorium giving a speech to teenagers. Not many in our noisy room paid much attention until his speech was over and the youth began to speak to the pope. By satellite transmission, young people from various parts of the country greeted John Paul with a gift. "Holy Father, we offer you the gift of our prayer.... We present you with the gift of our concern for others.... We come to you with the gift of our chastity."

Silence settled on our group, some of the world's most influential men and women. "We rejoice with you in this gift of music." Upon which an armless young man came to the stage in their amphitheater. Tony Melendez played a guitar with his toes and sang a song. The sight of Tony, lying on the stage and making music with the skill of a professional, entranced the leaders of the entertainment world and all the rest of us as well.

At his conclusion there was a roar of applause. John Paul, evidently moved, stood up and walked forward. He jumped off his platform and strode over to Melendez, saying in his broad Slavic voice, "Tony, Tony!" He embraced the young man who had no arms to hug him in return. The camera lingered on Tony's face, his eyes brimming, his appearance a picture of radiant joy.

In our ballroom, we were transfixed. People of all religions and none spontaneously let the quiet take hold of us. We had witnessed a transcendent moment that was nurtured by an experience of personal triumph over disability and our own sense of human solidarity. We remained in that healing silence for nearly ten minutes, until John Paul arrived and was greeted by an outpouring of warmth.

I will never forget that scene. A healing occurred there—not a miraculous restoration of a man's arms, but his marvelous touching of our hearts despite the awesome audience of a pope, thousands of teenagers and the sharp eyes of the entertainment establishment. I heard many of the famous people there say in various ways, "That young man has made me realize what really counts in life." We had glimpsed a humbling truth, well expressed by St. Paul: "I came to you in weakness and fear and much trembling,... but with a demonstration of spirit and power" (1 Corinthians 2:3, 4b).

Holistic Healing

The miracles of modern medicine rightly cause awe. We admire the genius of science and the skills of surgeons. Yet many people today also seek healing through such "alternative medicines" as acupuncture, chiropractic, biofeedback and herbal treatments. This reflects a hunger for holistic healing, the search for a personal touch—even a kind of spiritual encounter— that creates in us a sense of wholeness. The fact that science provides little proof of the effectiveness of these approaches means that the seekers choose such therapies in the spirit of human faith. The only evidence is anecdotal human testimony.

This experience echoes the search for holistic healing in the order of religious faith. Millions of people every year make pilgrimages to Lourdes and Medjugorje. Many explicitly go to these shrines for physical healings, or at least in the hope of seeing one. Relatively few ever experience a physical healing or witness one. Yet rare is the person who is disappointed by the pilgrimage. Almost everyone returns with such testimonies as: "I felt spiritually renewed." "My faith is strong again." "Jesus has become real to me."

As a boy I was touched by the film, *The Song of Bernadette*. Thirty years later, I stood at the grotto of Lourdes, immersed in the hymns of a believing community, listening to the rushing waters of the river Gave, visualizing the encounter of Bernadette and the Blessed Mother, gazing at the peaceful hope on the faces of the sick. I knew that faith was taking a deeper root in my heart. Jesus, my healer, was at work.

A close friend of mine, Boston pastor Father Neil Heery, made a pilgrimage to Medjugorje in the summer of 1987. He saw none of the wonders of which some others spoke, though he was present when the visionaries had their encounter with Mary. He shared with me a copy of his diary, in which he noted:

> We became acquainted with other members of our party. They came from Louisiana, Florida, Illinois, Texas, California, New York and Massachusetts. What began to make us a family was sharing with one another our reasons for coming to Medjugorje. For some it was to find answers to difficult problems. For others there was a longing desire for interior peace. Some may have simply come out of curiosity. What proved to be a graced experience for all was the support we gave one another.

Father Heery's testimony reflects the common experience that these shrines are places where spiritual healings occur more often than physical ones. In some cases the faith conversions are extraordinary; most are simply affirmations of a faith already in progress. Even when a sick person's body is not healed, the interior peace is considered a grace. This is a form of holistic healing at a religious level.

All this pertains to Jesus, my healer. The Gospel healing stories continue to make a striking impression on me. I love to see the lame man dancing to test his new legs, to listen to the blind man exclaim with almost drunken wonder at the colors of the universe, to smell the food cooking at Jairus' house as they prepare a resurrection feast for their daughter. I linger at the scene where a timid yet brave woman touches the hem of Christ's garment in the midst of a shoving crowd. More appealing is the warm hug Jesus gives her when her story is made public and she can go to the synagogue with her head held high again.

I watch with enduring fascination Jesus volubly taking to himself a leper, overcoming both physical repulsion and social mores to welcome this poor soul back to normal life. I share the abiding sense of danger on the shore of Gerasa, near the tombs, when Jesus confronts raw evil in the insanely powerful possessed man. Jesus risks his life to rescue this tortured man from his agony. I admire, with some envy, the sensitivity Jesus demonstrates when he goes through the motions of acting like a practitioner of folk medicine, using spit to make mud, using reassuring gestures to help the deaf to hear and the mute to speak.

The miracles of Jesus speak for themselves. More interesting are the words Jesus uses: "[A]s you have believed, let it be done for you." "Your faith has saved you." "Let it be done for you according to your faith" (Matthew 8:13b; 9:22b; 29b). Jesus intends to save the whole person, the spirit as well as the body. That is Christian holistic healing. Health in the spirit is as important as physical health in the body. Practitioners of alternative medicine claim that a wholesome mind leads to a wholesome body. Christian healing maintains that a wholesome faith in the heart has a positive effect on the total person.

What are some of the ways that Jesus, our healer, works in us today? I will speak here of just four powerful remedies that have a renewing effect on our whole personhood: letting go of our fears, concentrating on giving, finding the love within us and sharing our inner peace. I will take up in Chapter Seven his supreme form of healing—his gift of salvation, of which the healings covered here are specific effects.

When Jesus heals us he unfolds a potential for wholeness he has already planted within us as Son of God. Jesus never violates our unique makeup, as though he were adding something alien to our nature. Jesus our healer calls forth the health, wholeness and holiness that would already be flourishing if we had not let sin block our destiny and development. Jesus removes sin and all its children so that our self-transcending nature can soar like an eagle. He never does this without our consent. At the same time he is the lover whose affectionate invitation invites us to respond to him freely.

Let Go of Your Fears

When we are in touch with Jesus, he will heal our fears, selfishness, troubled hearts and grudging natures. His style is invitational.

God does not like to scare people. Scriptural accounts of heavenly manifestations—appearances of God or angels—always begin with the plea, "Do not be afraid." There is no Gospel record of Jesus trying to frighten anyone. God did not create fear. We manufactured it.

God made each of us a bundle of love energy designed for a life of self-transcendence. Today we marvel at how much energy can be locked up in an atom. We spend billions of dollars and our best brainpower to release that energy. We should therefore not be surprised that we are centers of unimagined energy. Sin interrupted and frustrated this original intention of God for us. Jesus Christ liberates us from sin's blockage of our true potential and frees us to become who we were meant to be in the first place. Christ's gifts of grace in the Church and the sacraments accomplish this purpose.

One of the basic healings we need is liberation from fear. In Galilee, Jerusalem and in our own situation Jesus finds us crippled by fear. Fear obscures our capacity for love. Fear tightens our hearts and makes us feel small and excessively cautious. Fear poisons our relationships, drives us to prove others wrong and make them feel inferior to us. Fear makes us see the world as divided.

Jesus comes to us to heal us from our fears of failure, rejection, pain and death. By doing so he liberates our capacity to love.

Fear of Failure

He looks at our fear of failure. This fear paralyzes us because we mistakenly believe that to *have* a failure is to *be* a failure. False ideas of success make this seem worse. Defining success in terms of wealth, power, fame, sexual conquest and popular acclaim distorts what our self-image really ought to be: namely, a person developing love, confidence, wisdom, courage, justice and mercy.

To be a person becoming more fully human by developing these qualities will, in the nature of things on earth, involve failure. No one succeeds in the real sense without failing. Look at the biographies of the saints—not just at the last chapter, where the saint is a finished product, but at the early chapters where the process of growth and conversion is recorded. Saints failed a lot. They made many mistakes.

Great saints knew how to fail colossally, pick up the pieces and move on. Peter failed Jesus three times in the courtyard of the high priest but let his tears of conversion lead him to the beach at Galilee, where he exploded in love for his dearest friend, Jesus, three times (see John 21:15-19). Paul failed miserably when he involved himself in the judicial murder of Christians. His failure tormented him but did not prevent his conversion to Christ. So great a stepping-stone to self-transcendence were his failures that eventually he witnessed and composed the greatest poem on love ever written (see 1 Corinthians 13:1-13).

When Jesus sees us trapped by our fear of failure,

he quietly shows us the marks of the wounds in his body. He, the risen One, kept what seemed to be the signs of failure on his glorified flesh. They were steps on the road to glory. Jesus has the key to unlock the handcuffs in our souls. All we need to do is ask him to use it, and rest assured that he loves to heal us of our fear of failure.

Fear of Rejection

Jesus calls us to self-transcendence. This means becoming who we are meant to be, to have a true realization of our God-given potential. Imagine Jesus as an archer holding a bow and arrow. Each of us is the arrow. He aims us at God, the absolute center of love and the source of our true happiness. If we permit him to release us from his bow, we—the "arrows"—will soar toward our proper fulfillment.

But fear holds us back. Not just fear of failure but also fear of rejection. Without a doubt, rejection hurts. Others bloody us with repudiation, disdain and callous treatment. This pain is deeper when it is received from friends and loved ones. Betrayals depress us and increase our caution about relationships. Fear of rejection breeds timidity about getting involved with others.

What are we to do? Take the fear of rejection and let it go. Symbolically drop it in the nearest river and let it float out to sea and be lost. The only force binding this fear to our hearts is our own decision to keep it there. Ask Jesus to take it from us and dissolve it in his love. He will heal us from our fear of rejection because he is the one Lover who will never betray us.

Fear of Pain

In 1963, on the Wednesday before Palm Sunday, I was in St. Peter's Basilica to attend an audience with Pope John XXIII. He had only three months to live. He was still rotund, but his color was pale and his face lined with pain. Yet he smiled broadly and his eyes cheerfully gazed at us. He seemed very much at home, mainly because the twenty thousand people there were mostly from his home area of Sotto Il Monte. Friends and neighbors had come to bid their dear friend a warm good-bye.

He spoke about his joyful childhood memories and of the people's present hardships on the small farms where most of them worked. He said, "I know the difficulties you face. Just remember that above all your doors is a cross. I have one on my desk. When I am beset by pain I look at Jesus and say, 'They did it to you. They will do it to me. So what's the complaining?'"

He did not ask to have pain taken away. His prayer always concentrated on not running away from the pain that life and growth inevitably bring. He prayed to Jesus to be liberated from *fear* of the pain that accompanies human and spiritual development.

Jesus was not immune to the fear of pain. At Gethsemane he experienced dread of the suffering that lay ahead of him. He asked God to take it away. But then he surrendered to his Father's will and overcame his fear of pain. Love conquered fear and led him to his greatest accomplishment, the salvation of the world.

Some pain is unavoidable in life. What can be

avoided is the fear of pain, especially when it stops us from loving. Christ's third act of healing is to free us from that fear, if we let him.

Fear of Death

Closely related to the fear of pain is the primordial fear of death. The deepest of all human feelings is the love for life, the desire to keep on living even when a sea of troubles besieges us. The will to live is a powerful force. This accounts for the very human fear of dying and death. Such fear takes the form of denial of death.

Denial of death prevents us from benefiting from the positive value of facing the reality of our own death. Courageously meditating on our own death can help us become alive to the possibilities of living. When done with faith, this reflection draws us to think of eternal life. Performed with wisdom, this thoughtful look at death motivates us to fill our days with love, care and moral concern for others. The record of Jesus, the martyrs and the saints is of people who released themselves from the fear of death.

Euthanasiasts seem to have overcome this fear of death. This is an illusion. They argue that living is not the most desirable good because the quality of life is more important than its quantity. They say we should die with dignity. We should exert rational control over our dying, either by suicidal ingestion of drugs or by doctor-assisted termination (which is simply murder). But, in a certain sense, there is no good death. Death is undignified. It is the indignity of dying that troubles many people. In actuality, the euthanasia movement is another form of death denial. Its supporters exhibit both the fear of pain and the fear of death.

Jesus saw the value of his death as opening for us the transition to eternal life. But Jesus envisioned death itself as a sorrowful moment. He trembled with anger at the tomb of Lazarus, thinking of how sin caused death and what sorrow death engenders. He shuddered at Gethsemane when he looked starkly at his own forthcoming death. The Church's funeral rites never ignore the dreadful side of death, even as they point us joyfully to the heavenly life beyond.

The sooner we are released from the fear of death, the quicker will our faith grow in the Christian possibilities of this life. A real Christian is a life-affirmer. We will also begin to experience the Kingdom of Jesus sooner here on earth because we will have looked through death's door to our final destiny.

Jesus, my healer, will liberate me from the four fears: fear of failure, rejection, pain and death. In each instance the result is an increase of my capacity to love. The expulsion of fear is the beginning of love.

Concentrate on Giving

Everyone loves getting. But the best way to get is to give. As the Prayer of St. Francis says, "It is in giving that we receive." We love to be strong. The day we decide to help others to have strength, we suddenly find power filling our own souls.

We want to overcome the confusion in our lives

and concentrate our scattered energies. We hunger for stability and seek to put our lives in order. The moment we assist others to find stability in their lives, we begin to receive the gift of stability in our own. As we help other persons dispel the demon of confusion that plagues them, we notice clarity emerging in our own spirits. When we offer our time, talent and treasure to help friends gather their scattered energies, we will be delighted to experience the unification of our own energies. Giving is like a boomerang. We offer a spiritual value to someone else and it comes back to us. Giving is receiving.

Do you want to be attractive? Then make other people feel appealing. Help them to walk tall and flourish with hope. Endow them with dignity. Shower them with an appreciation of their own wonder, beauty and worth. The secret of becoming attractive is to expend our energies in bringing out the goodness in others. Every act of increasing another's beauty automatically causes our own growth in attractiveness.

Do we languish because we are misunderstood? Are we depressed because no one understands us? The solution is found in understanding others, seeing the good points in what they say, giving them the benefit of the doubt. Are we adult thumb-suckers, angry at the world for not consoling us when we want some comfort? The way out of this black hole is to give compassion to those who are in pain, to sit with the lonely and to let them see our tears of sympathy for them.

Just one miracle occurs in all the Gospels: the multiplication of the loaves. Why did the Gospel writers insist on reporting this event? Yes, it was an example of Christ's concern for hungry people. Indeed, it was a sign that pointed to the reality and meaning of the Eucharist. But surely it was also a reminder of Christ's invitation to be a giver. Bread is multiplied in the giving. Hoard the bread and it will grow stale and diminish. Constantly give away the bread of strength, stability, energy, clarity and attractiveness to others and it will multiply both in others and in ourselves. The gift of love inside us is multiplied, not lost, when we give it away. The only way to get is to give.

Social critics have loudly noted the scourge of individualism in our society. The result is an excess of greed and me-centeredness. Jesus, our healer, knows this and is ready to cure us of this affliction. He sees us standing behind the barricades of self-absorption. He gazes at our fists, grasping the little we have. In his hands is a gift of gold that says, "Giving is receiving." He knows that sin has blinded us to our true potential. He would be delighted to help us see, to help us to open our hands and take his gift. His approach is invitational and lovingly insistent. When we open ourselves to him, we will be healed. Nothing can make us happier.

Find the Love That Is Within You

We are all aware that we have a hunger drive. At least three times a day we have the urge to eat—and, alas for our weight control, often more than that. We are also acutely conscious that we have a sex drive. And we are not likely to forget it in a culture that constantly reminds us of it in ads, films, TV shows, novels and surveys.

We have another drive inside us that may be less apparent but just as real. This is our God-given love drive. Theologian Bernard Lonergan describes this as an unrestricted drive to love and be loved. Of course we are aware that we hunger for affection from others. Are we as alert to our inner dynamic push to love other people? We can get in touch with this source of love energy and release it. Nothing makes us feel more free than when we activate this love drive and pour it out on the world. If fear makes us perceive the world as nothing but divisions, then love will enable us to see the world as a potential unity in God. This perception causes us to bring harmony to ourselves, our family and our world. Those who only see life as fractious will make it more so. Mischievous people cause mischief. Those who have a vision of life as a unity will make unification happen.

Each person we meet is an opportunity for love from us right now. Little will be gained from worrying about that person's past or future, whether they deserve our love because of the life they have lived or whether they will waste the love we give. Without worrying about such things, we should love them simply, directly and without guile. The best strategy is to enjoy heart-to-heart communion with them. Even when they do not accept our love, that will not stop the harmony we have sent into the world; it will already have caused a growth of love within ourselves. Love is a positive reality; non-love is a vacuum. Love is a presence; non-love is an absence. It is obvious that love is better.

Every day we must remove blocks to love. How can we do this? We have already taken the first step when we let go of our fear of failure, rejection, pain and death. St. Augustine says that prayer and meditation are excellent ways to remove the blocks to our awareness of and capacity for love. When our prayer becomes a friendly conversation with Jesus, the dialogue uncovers our dynamic love drive. In awakening our hunger for nothing less than the God who *is* love, we discover how energetic our ability to love really is.

When Jesus encountered the Samaritan woman at the well, he helped her shed her fears and become aware of her deep love drive. He dug a well in her self-awareness. When she sensed this gift, she felt a divine spring burst through her inner self, a "spring of water welling up" (John 4:14b).

Jesus, our healer, realizes that we have this extraordinary love drive inside us. After all, as Son of God, he put it there. "All things came to be through him..." (John 1:3a). We already have this gift. All we need is to notice it is there. Jesus will happily dig a well in our awareness so we can get in touch with our love drive. Ask him for this and prepare for one of life's most pleasant surprises.

Then we will praise God for this most divine of all gifts. We will take this love and pour it into each act of our day. Great genius and art pay attention to the smallest detail. Spiritual art is putting love into the smallest act as well as the greatest one. It means meeting each person every day with affection, ease and love.

Share Your Inner Peace

On the four hundredth anniversary of the death of
John of the Cross, I attended a one-man show about
him in the crypt of the National Shrine of the
Immaculate Conception in Washington, D.C.
Beforehand, I wondered how the actor, Leonardo de
Fillipis, would ever be able to hold our attention for
ninety minutes. What would he do? Would he take us
through the mystical poetry or the "dark night" of
John's soul? Was it possible to make this available to
an audience?

As it turned out, the actor chose to take us
through John's life from his birth up to his escape
from the Carmelite prison in Toledo. He wore the
brown Carmelite habit and the cream-colored choir
cape. The setting in the crypt chapel, one of
Washington's architectural jewels, with its low vaults,
dreamy golds and subtle mosaics, was a tranquil
environment that suited the meditation. Leonardo
used his skills to bring dialogues alive, especially
when Madre Teresa first met Friar John, upon whom
she built her hopes for a reform of the male
contingent of the Order. "But he looks so small, so
thin, so young!" (She was 52 and he was 25.)

We heard the poetry of John sung to Spanish
melodies throughout the presentation. Best of all, we
heard some verses of his poem, "The Dark Night," in
connection with John's imprisonment. His external
situation fed him the imagery for describing his
spiritual journey. After his escape, John finds refuge
in a Carmelite nunnery. As the nuns sing to him, he
rallies from the tragic situation in which he had found

himself and performs a dance that puts us in touch with his inner joy.

I share this story with you for several reasons: First, the actor appeared to be more than a skillful imitator. He communicated his own religious faith. Second, he unveiled the remarkable inner peace of John of the Cross. And we were all affected by John's peace as though he were present with us that evening.

It is not easy to experience inner peace today. Our hearts want peace, but our heads won't let us alone. Our heads are like a twenty-four-hour movie. The show never stops. The tapes keep playing. Upsets, troubles and tragedies cling to our minds like arthritic deposits. These rough commanders of our attention trouble us and threaten any hope for inner peace.

If we want to have inner peace, we must first release our mind from its mental debates. As in the case of our fears, the first step we might take to rid ourselves of these disturbers of our peace is to drop them into an imaginary stream that dissolves them in the ocean. We may be too fond of our anxieties. Holding onto them heals nothing. Letting them go begins the process of gaining inner peace.

Then we should treat ourselves to some quiet time each day. Stop the world and get off for a while. People burn out when they forget this simple advice. The modern craze for efficiency has often resulted in putting a lot of energy into little things. The truly efficient person expends small energy for small acts and has plenty left for the big challenges. Quiet time restores energy.

Finally, discover the old truth that peace does not result from good behavior. If this were so, why do so many people with correct behavior complain that they have no peace in their hearts? Instead, truly good behavior, the kind that causes goodness in others, *follows* peace.

At the Last Supper, Jesus promised to give us inner peace (see John 14:27). To receive that we need to bind ourselves to him as intimately as a vine to a branch. When peace flows like a river from Christ, the vine, into us, the branches, we produce the grapes of loving behavior. To carry the comparison further, we create an environment that has the "wine" of joy. This fourth healing from Jesus is his gift of inner peace.

Conclusion

As the Gospels show, Jesus, my healer, can cure the body and the soul. In this meditation I have shown four ways in which Jesus acts as the healer of our inner life today. Our divine physician says to us:

1) Let go of your fears of failure, rejection, pain and death.

2) Concentrate on giving.

3) Find the love that is within you.

4) Share your inner peace.

Through the power of the Holy Spirit within us, these healing words of Jesus accomplish what they say— provided we are open to change. Jesus is on our side.

He wants us to have these gifts. He will love away all obstacles to their reception. He will even show us the appeal of these choices and edge us toward the openness we need.

We will be pleased with the results which free up our capacity to love, increase our enthusiasm about being givers and make us a source of peace for those we meet.

Reflection

Jesus, our healer, is interested in our happiness and spiritual health. He will be more effective in healing us when we stay in regular, personal touch with him. The following suggestions are ways to open ourselves to the four powerful remedies considered in this chapter. Try one of these exercises each day.

Banishing Fear

List your fears, both physical and emotional, of failure, rejection, pain and death. Pick the ones that trouble you most. Place them in the hands of Jesus and ask him to drop them into a stream where they will float away and no more be seen or felt. Repeat this each day until you feel the grip of these fears loosen and disappear.

Recall that each person you meet also struggles with fears. Make that person feel at ease with you. Remove any threat you might bring. As you help them to meet you without fear, your own fears will diminish.

At the beginning of each hour, repeat Christ's heartwarming invitation, "Be not afraid." This serves as a Christian mantra to keep you aware of your goal of losing your fear by means of the grace and power of Jesus.

Improving Your Capacity to Give

Name three values you wish you had in your life. For example: personal responsibility, a sense of purpose, a positive outlook. Think of ways to impart these gifts, quietly and sensitively, to people you meet. Invite Jesus to be near you in each encounter so that his graciousness will affect yours. Remember that each gift to another gives birth to that same gift in yourself.

Investigate the needs of your local community as well as society at large: the homeless, poor children, AIDS victims, people with chemical addictions, etc. Practice charitable giving with your time, your talents and/or your treasure.

The Prayer of St. Francis, "Lord, make me an instrument of your peace," contains ten petitions. Adopt one petition each day as a spiritual guideline for your behavior. Each evening evaluate how well you lived by the specific guideline for the day.

Getting in Touch With Your Love Drive

At the end of each day examine how well you related to other people. Were you afraid to show love to someone? Did you love until it hurt? If you refused love to someone, what was the reason? What will you do tomorrow to improve your ability to love?

Look at St. Paul's First Letter to the Corinthians. His meditation on love (13:1-13) has thirteen verses. Take one verse each morning as a theme for your behavior that day. Review the results in the evening.

Each evening think of the love you received from people that day. Praise God for each gift and pray for the intentions of those who showed you love.

Sharing Your Inner Peace

Visualize the room where the apostles gathered on Easter night (see John 20:19-23). Feel their fear. See the risen Jesus appear to them. Hear him say, not once but twice, "Peace be with you." Then hear Jesus say those words to you. Quietly repeat his words until they envelop you.

Each time you hear people fostering and talking of discord, division, hostility, think of ways to draw them toward the desire for peace and harmony.

Set aside at least ten minutes a day to be still and quiet. Ask Jesus to give you his peace.

Prayer

Jesus, my healer, your Gospel witness shows that you
are interested in the total health of each human being.
By saving us from our sins, you set in motion the
healing of our souls from fear of failure, rejection,
pain and death. You also offer gifts that help us
become givers, discover our love drives and acquire
inner peace. These inner healings have a positive
effect on our bodies as well as a wholesome impact on
all our relationships with others.

I praise you for your healing presence and thank you
for the healing I have received from you. At the same
time I know that I will need your healing power all my
life. Rest your healing hand upon me and let your
power make me whole.

Chapter Three

JESUS, MY TEACHER

The Master of Meditation

During a visit to Singapore, I was taken on a tour of
the city by a young Singaporean of Chinese origin. He
brought me to the Botanical Gardens and led me to
the orchid display. He left me alone to wander among
the orchid plants, to feast on their rainbow of colors
and wonder about such an extravagance of beauty
that would soon perish. Soon after that he guided me
to the rose garden.

I remarked, "These gardens are havens for
meditation." He looked surprised and replied, "You
are the first westerner I have ever heard mention
meditation. Do you meditate every day? How long do
you meditate?" I told him that I meditate each
morning and evening. He confided that he meditates
each day as long as it takes a chopstick to burn—
about an hour.

Some time later I was in San Diego to give a
conference to Catholic chaplains at the naval base. I
was invited to attend the recruits' Mass. There a
thousand eighteen- to twenty-one-year-olds in the
middle of their basic training exhibited the immense
enthusiasm of youth in the way they sang the hymns

and boisterously participated in the worship.

The base chaplain was a young Franciscan priest who wore his habit—for "vocational awareness," as he put it. After Communion he spoke to the troops. "It's time for the catacomb exercise. Sit up straight. Put your feet flat on the floor. Place your hands on your knees. Close your eyes. Go into the catacomb, the quiet place deep inside you. Let peace possess you. Let Jesus be the center of your attention." All of us followed his guidance and a restful mood of faith soothed us. The experience reminded me of the story where Elijah heard God's voice not in the noise of thunder and earthquake, but in the whispered silence (see 1 Kings 19:11-13).

Jesus as Meditation Master

These meditation experiences are small hints of the great inner world each of us has. They are awakenings to the possibilities of our inner journey and pertinent to a reflection on Jesus as teacher. One way of speaking of Jesus as my teacher is to view him as my meditation master. As I roam through the pages of the Gospel and listen to Jesus, the teacher, I find him always leading his hearers (and me) to move within and explore the world of the spirit.

Over the years I have thought of Jesus as my teacher in a variety of ways. I have seen him as an interpreter of Scripture, drawing out its true meaning, as he did in the Sermon on the Mount and similar teaching moments. I have viewed him as an artful preacher who used stories from everyday life to

capture the imagination of his listeners so he could
drive home a point about this or that gospel principle.
Often I conceived of him as a patient instructor
imparting moral maxims and spiritual advice.
Frequently I imagined him as a skillful exhorter to
proper Christian behavior.

Gradually my appreciation of Jesus as a teacher
of meditation emerged. In a number of ways he
approaches us as a meditation master. Jesus looked at
his "students" as centers of mystery, not problems to
be solved. He found us all in self-made dark tunnels of
sinfulness and invited us to come into the light.
Paradoxically, he did this by sending us inside to
investigate ourselves, our attitudes, our approaches
to life. In other words he was urging us to develop our
capacity for meditative prayer.

I began to see that his sermons are not only
coherent explanations of how to be moral or spiritual,
but also a series of sayings, each of which can enable
us to discover within ourselves the drive toward God.
He is indeed teaching us eternal truths which are
meant to shape our minds, but he also leads us to the
meditative prayer of the heart. His magnificent
parables are designed more to wake up our spirits
than to captivate our attention. More than stories with
a moral, they are powerful images meant to open up
truths about ourselves which lie hidden within. Each
parable turns on a light inside our consciousness.

His word is a seed dropped into the well of my
awareness. Its growth depends on how willingly I
permit divine power to make it grow. The Good
Samaritan is a potential ideal hidden within me if only
I allow God to activate it. The Prodigal Son is me the

day I stop denying the possibility of forgiveness, that gift from God sown into my consciousness.

Jesus, then, is not explaining mystery but illuminating it by helping us to see it within ourselves. His teachings and stories, therefore, become revelations of what God has planted within our hearts about who we are and who we are called to be. That is why Jesus says the Kingdom of God is within us (see Luke 17:21). Jesus tries to help us accept our personal mystery and discover how it can unfold and influence our thinking, attitudes and behavior.

Trappist Abbot Thomas Keating illustrates this with a useful image. He envisions the human spirit as a river. The surface is our stream of consciousness, the twenty-four-hour inside movie of our thoughts, memories, imaginations, resentments, hurts, pleasures, victories, concerns, mental debates and mind games. Keating calls this the psychological level of awareness.

Beneath this busy flow of inner traffic is the deeper and more peaceful world of the spirit. Here is the spiritual world of consciousness. Meditation's first goal is to probe beneath the surface of our river into this realm of spirit. Here we are less affected by the noise of both the outer world and of our surface concerns.

Deeper yet is the stillpoint of our spirit. This is the contact point with God. Here is the divine indwelling, the Holy Spirit toward whom we journey and with whom we converse and from whom we receive God-given energy.

Some years ago an Anglican bishop, John Robinson, complained that we think of God too physically as "up there," too far away from daily life, too much a sky God. He said we would be better off conceiving of God as the "ground of our being," a God who is right here.

I think he had a valid point, except he found an inadequate solution. His "ground of being" was still too abstract, a vague something behind all the hubbub here on earth. Instead of being the puppeteer arranging life's interactions from the sky, this God is down here somewhere holding matters together. If I am not supposed to pray to a sky God, abstract and removed from earth, why should I be content with devotion to a ground God equally impersonal and fuzzy?

The Son of God has already solved this dilemma by leaving the remote sanctuary of heaven to walk with us on earth. Jesus as teacher tried to evoke in each person he met an awareness of the inner life and the possibilities of encountering the divine force within us. God is certainly right here, personally present to each human being at the very source of each person's spirit, ready to be living and active in the adventure of the soul.

The Teacher as Storyteller

When I entered the seminary of St. Norbert Abbey many years ago, I had only the vaguest idea of my calling to the priesthood and religious life. During my years of formation I had two "awakening experiences," conversion moments. Each instance was caused by a powerful story.

The first event occurred during my novitiate, when I read *The Story of a Soul*, the autobiography of St. Therese Martin of Lisieux. I had never expected that the story of a Carmelite nun from a country, a culture and a way of life so different from anything I had known could have such a profound impact on me. When she spoke of the love of Jesus, I found her words resonating in my own heart. I had not imagined that I possessed the potential for such inner experience. How did she do this? Precisely through the powerful story of her spiritual adventure. She shared her love of Jesus and awoke in me the same response. Her graceful story initiated me into a spiritual journey. Her "little way" taught me how to make my ordinary actions expressions of love for God, others and self. As a storyteller, she was also a teacher showing how I could discover the mystery of God present within myself.

Toward the end of my seminary training, I heard another story that was equally compelling and life-changing. During our meals someone read inspirational books to us. Most of the time the voice of the reader and the content of the book were just background music to the subdued clatter of silverware and dishes while the food was being consumed. Rarely did it absorb our youthful attention. We lent minimal, dutiful attention.

Then one day the reader started *The Seven Storey Mountain*, by Thomas Merton. At first his story solicited a keener attention because the prose was so superior and the anecdotes about New York City so full of human interest. Within a few days it was clear we were hearing a compelling spiritual drama, a conversion narrative that was unique and riveting. Never before or since has our abbey dining room been so silent. Merton's story wrapped us all in a state of communal attention and caused an unprecedented spiritual awakening. His words cast a spell because he was so spiritually alive and made us feel the same possibility.

In retrospect, I am glad that I heard his story in that communal setting before I read it in the solitude of my room. His story released a contagious faith energy among us. We had heard about transcendence in our theology classes. Listening to his remarkable story at a monastery table helped us experience it. We thrived on each other's interest in what he revealed. His story had the effect of magic, but was far better than that because it was an evocation of real mystery.

If I were to single out the enduring effect of that memorable encounter, it is the commitment to meditation that Merton's story stimulated. His celebration of meditation, his ability to make it believable and worthwhile have remained with me all these years. I periodically return to Merton's writings to regain my faltering motivation to stay with silent prayer. His personal story has remained an inspiration to me whenever I stray from the well within where I can meet God's Spirit and the waters of new life.

Therese Martin and Thomas Merton both spoke from their respective cloisters about getting in touch with the mystery of God within us no matter where we live. I cite these two compelling storytellers because I believe they exemplify what Jesus, my teacher, did in his parables. How was he to describe the secret drama of his own interior life? How could he portray the future that he promised us? He chose his parables about the Kingdom of heaven, his own spiritual life story, to reveal a glimpse of his inner life. At the same time his stories startled listeners into perceiving spiritual realities within themselves that they had not recognized before. The seed, the pearl, the grain of wheat, the vine, the banquet—all are images that stir self-revelations, openings to who we are and our destinies.

When we share our own stories of conversion, we often find ourselves reaching for poetry, metaphor and imagery to describe our encounter with the divine. If we examine instances of our own self-disclosures, we are as apt as Jesus was to tell our story with a touch of mystery. Only the poetry of life seems equal to expressing the joy of loving and being loved by God.

Miracle as Contemplative Moment

Jesus taught by his deeds as well as his words. He lived what he said. This not only lent credibility to his teaching but also produced a similar result: The force of his personal presence itself aroused inner awareness. Someone so alive to his own spiritual depth made others conscious of their own. I came to realize that more when I appreciated why John's Gospel calls the miracles "signs."

The Synoptics (Matthew, Mark and Luke) dwell on miracles as acts of mercy and compassion, which indeed they are. John knew that, too, but saw that they fulfilled yet another purpose. John calls them signs that disclose the glory of Jesus. *Glory* is a biblical term that describes God's making the divine presence felt in the world. For John, a miracle unveiled the mysterious inner presence of Jesus.

The miracle, then, is a moment of intimacy in which Jesus shares his remarkable inner life with us. The miracle also alerts the viewers to the pleasant surprise of the potential in their own interior space. As a meditation master, Jesus uses the effect of his personal presence and the sharing of his intimate life in miracles in order to draw us inward.

Hence by his sayings and parables, his warm presence and self-revelation, Jesus undertakes the admittedly challenging task of waking us up from the dreamlike trance in which the world's busyness engulfs us.

The Bread Is a Person

John 6 vividly demonstrates what I have been saying here about Jesus as my teacher and meditation master. The scene opens at the northern shore of the lake of Galilee, where it is relatively narrow. Jesus, needing some quiet place to pray after an intense healing ministry, sails with the apostles to the other side of the lake.

The crowd which had journeyed to Capernaum to see him decides to follow on foot. It takes them about three hours to circle the upper shore and meet him on the eastern coast. From his boat Jesus can see the column of eager marchers, singing pilgrim psalms, impulsively drawn to him, straining forward to be with one who responded to their hopes and needs. They are no longer sheep without a shepherd. They have discovered their shepherd in Jesus.

The two groups converge at the eastern shore. Jesus leads them up a nearby mountain. There is no record of what Jesus says, but since it is Passover he perhaps leads them in a meditation on the meaning of the feast. It must be a prolonged time of prayer. So absorbed are all of them in the divine mystery that they have no time to find food for their evening meal. In response to their need, Jesus multiplies the loaves and fishes.

So significant is this miracle that it is found in all four Gospels and twice in two of them (Matthew 14:13-21; 15:32-39; Mark 6:32-44; 8:1-10; Luke 19:10-17; John 6:1-15). The Synoptics report the miracle as an example of Christ's thoughtfulness about hungry people and an inspiration to all of us to follow Jesus in feeding the hungry and poor. In John's Gospel, however, the bread miracle is called a sign of the glory-presence of Jesus. Through it, Jesus shares with us his inner life and intends to make us think of our own.

This becomes clear in the dialogue about the bread miracle which occurs soon afterward (John 6:22-71). In the gathering space in front of the Capernaum synagogue, Jesus initiates a Christian meditation process that flows from the people's experience of the bread miracle. Jesus leads them through four steps explained below. (I should mention that these are general stages of meditation, not techniques or method. Many methods are available to suit personal temperaments and situations. Such methods include centering prayer, the Ignatian Method, the Benedictine "Lectio Divina," popular devotions, etc., that lead into silent reflection.

Look Beyond Religious Literalism

The people have misinterpreted the bread miracle in two ways. First, they perceived it in political terms and sought to make Jesus their messianic king. He rebuffed their claims and fled from their rallying cries. Now, in a calmer mood, they decide that at least he can be a cult figure to whom they will surrender themselves. If he will not be a politician filling their stomachs, then he can be a guru warming their religious emotions.

Just as he would not be their king, Jesus rejects their new form of passive dependence on him. Jesus does not seek spiritual parasites but human beings alive to their own spiritual cosmos. Jesus wants dynamic relationships, not people who will cling to him and try to force him to practice spiritual paternalism. He will be neither a mood-satisfier nor a stomach-filler.

Urging them to talk about their experience of the bread miracle, he hears them compare it to the manna miracle that God provided in Israel's desert days. Jesus drew their attention to the transitoriness of both the manna and the bread: Once eaten, either is gone—and they are hungry again.

He will offer them another kind of bread. When they eat it, they will begin to taste eternal life. They need God bread, love bread. Jesus charms them with the vision of such a bread. He warms them with the offer of love. They are moved to beg him for this bread. Jesus has inched them away from politics and religious paternalism, from the externals of life. He has opened them to experience their own spiritual potential. He will play an essential part in that experience—as the next step illustrates.

Meet Jesus as a Person

"Jesus said to them, 'I am the bread of life...' " (John 6:35a). The bread is the image of the person. He directly introduces them to the powerful mystery that is the real purpose of his encounter with them. They think of him as a carpenter, a preacher and a healer. They realize he will not be a politician and now he is refusing the religious role they have designed for him. They are also puzzled and shocked by his application of the sacred expression "I AM" to himself. When Moses had asked the name of the person who spoke to him from the burning bush, he had heard these words "I AM," the name of God (see Exodus 3:4-15).

Jesus does not try to explain the mystery he has revealed to them. Instead, he intensifies his personal appeal to them. "Believe in me. Trust me. Come to me," he says, in effect. He is asking for love. He appeals to them to shed the self-interest that has brought them to him. Love has the inner light that helps one to accept truth and appreciate mystery. By showing them how vitally alive he is, he hopes to stimulate in them a sense of how marvelously alive they are. When they discover that about themselves, they will have a love affair with him and feel at home with the mystery of God, who has come so close to them.

Be Broken

A meditation process begins with a regular withdrawal from the fascinations of public life and even from the fantasies on the surface of our inner river. The next step is to get in touch with the mystery of the person, especially Jesus. Jesus has taken his hearers through these two steps. The third stage is breaking away from the hold that selfishness, the superficial, sinfulness and the transient have upon us. It is like breaking a wild horse so that its sturdy power may have a true direction. The brokenness I speak of here is not the kind that leads one to passivity and sheepishness. I am talking about a breakdown that leads to a breakthrough.

It is just such a stage that Jesus introduces at Capernaum. He knows that anyone who embarks on meditative self-discovery allied to a relationship with him must make a courageous decision. They must break away from what they have known and risk doing so. He knows that he will cause a conflict within them. He honors their drive toward nobility and courage even as he risks surfacing their wish to be evasive and weak, to choose fear and flight.

He uses the language of Eucharist to move them to a new depth of mystery and a fresh area of choice. It has often been noted that John recounts no institution of the Eucharist in his Last Supper account. Instead, he reports the Bread of Life dialogue as the setting for this revelation. Jesus reveals his teaching on Eucharist at the threshold of an ancient Capernaum synagogue. The context is his meditation process and his offer of personal communion with those people. He uses direct supernatural probing to open them to mystery and courage.

"For my flesh is true food, and my blood is true drink. Whoever eats my flesh and drinks my blood remains in me and I in him" (John 6:55-56). Some today wonder whether Jesus would have delivered such a remarkable challenge to those people. Could they have been prepared? I would argue that he did and they were. They were heirs of the cumulative faith of over a thousand years of covenant living. They were accustomed to revelation and the prophets' power to stir up their faith when it cooled. They had also been stimulated by the preaching, miracles and extraordinary presence of Jesus. They were culturally and spiritually ready to be challenged. They were also free to accept or reject what Jesus invited them to do.

Jesus knew that people are stronger than they seem. The human spirit is more receptive to divine mystery than the advocates of hesitancy contend. God made the soul to desire the divine. Jesus did not fear spiritual overload. He had a great respect for the human capacity to accept him. In speaking about the brokenness that goes with eucharistic living, Jesus was also addressing the general brokenness which will accompany the commitment to an inner life. In both cases people can expect to be broken in order to love and be loved. Ultimately, their new life would make salvation and love available to the world through the power of Jesus.

Jesus does not spare his listeners this third stage. He is doing more than asking them to assent to a eucharistic doctrine—though he indeed does that. His more insistent challenge is to their lives. Can they live through the brokenness that Eucharist implies? Can they persevere in the inner journey that will include a breakdown that leads to a breakthrough?

Accept Jesus

The people had encountered someone so spiritually alive that they became aware of their own inner possibilities. Jesus had charisma. Not the kind that bulldozes others into blissful submission; he projected a penetrating warmth. Jesus made sure that his immense attractiveness liberated people to be themselves. He had no intention of mesmerizing them or tricking them into a decision that was not wholly free. He met them soul to soul.

Now Jesus has done enough. The Word goes into silence. He has not been argumentative. Love, not logic, is his strategy. His silence in the afternoon of a faith encounter at Capernaum permits them to come to their own decisions. The quiet of the sun in the west and the companionable surf of Galilee contrasts with their inner drama.

At first they enjoy the consciousness-raising Jesus had evoked in them. Yes, they should get beyond life's externals. Indeed, they ought to treat a person as a mystery. But to be broken? For many of them the price was too great. "This saying is hard" (John 6:60b).

To their credit, they really do appreciate what he

invites them to do. They understand the life change required and decide it is too difficult, too risky. In their intuitions they behold the dream he holds out for them. But fear and flight intervene. They reject the vision and therefore the spiritual adventure that would have led to it. Even his promise that they will be sustained by his love in the process does not convince them. They prefer the hot prison of the moment to the liberation that can be theirs.

Jesus asks the Twelve what they have decided. Peter answers for all of them, "Master, to whom shall we go? You have the words of eternal life. We have come to believe and are convinced that you are the Holy One of God" (John 6:68b-69). It is an astonishing affirmation of the Eucharist as well as of the divinity and messiahship of Jesus. Just as Peter was inspired by the Holy Spirit at Caesarea Phillipi to make a faith commitment to Jesus (see Matthew 16:16), so here again the Spirit of God touches a deep chord in Peter and elicits his heartfelt response. It is exactly moments of illumination like this that one can expect from a person who has stayed with the faith journey in meditation.

My teacher, Jesus, continues to call me and all of us to surrender to him as Bread of Life. Additionally, he invites us to daily Christian meditation. He reaches out to us from Capernaum to the present moment to the last second of recorded time.

Reflection

Jesus, my teacher, is my spiritual master. If I have come to him, it is because the Father has drawn me. Jesus has sent me the Holy Spirit who dwells at the stillpoint of my soul to help me with my prayer.

Daily meditation is a valued way of getting in touch with Jesus as my teacher and the Spirit as my enabler. A widely used approach to Christian meditation is centering prayer. Spiritual writers provide slight variations on how to do this. The following general steps seem to work best for most people:

Prepare Yourself

Choose a regular time each morning and evening, but not too soon after a meal. Plan on twenty-minute periods. Find a zone of silence. Pick a comfortable position, one that relaxes you while at the same time allows you to stay alert. Many suggest being seated, back straight, with hands peacefully resting.

Visualize your inner life as a river. Your preoccupations ride boisterously on its surface. Beneath it is your deeper spirit, the place where you can find calm. At your inmost point is the holy place where the Spirit dwells, drawing you to Jesus and love.

Read a passage from Scripture, out loud and slowly. Think of the scriptural words as spoken to you personally by Jesus. Pick a word, a phrase or a brief sentence that you will use to gather yourself into the presence of Jesus and make yourself open to his loving influence. Once you select this prayer, do not change it during the meditation. Calmly say it whenever you need to refocus on Jesus.

Rest Within Yourself

Allow the prayer text to take you on your inner journey. The busy traffic on the surface of your spirit will attract your attention. Feelings, images, mental debates, arguments, mind games, hurts, resentments, thoughts about what lies ahead or what happened that day will clamor for your attention. Let them go. Do not fight them. Struggling against them is like wearing Chinese handcuffs: The more you resist, the tighter they squeeze your wrists. Teresa of Avila calls them the "monkeys of the mind," who deserve little more than a playful smile as you move into the prayer level beneath the surface. Return to your prayer text and let it carry you into the deep.

It is here that Christ's advice about discipleship becomes more meaningful. He says, "Lose your self. Take your cross. Follow me" (see Luke 9:23). This is a good time for losing yourself. Let go of your ambition to control—your power needs. Let go of your yearning to be admired, esteemed, loved. Let go of your hunger for security and survival. Dying to them will lead you to a rising that enriches you with them in Jesus. Meditation is thus a Way of the Cross that leads to your personal Easter.

Discover your inner home where the space is so vast there is room to welcome the world—and the immensity of God. Welcome Jesus.

Resolve to Be and Become

At the conclusion of your meditation, recall that your future is a matter of being and becoming, not doing. This is not a time to resolve agenda or choose some action. That belongs to another aspect of your life, related indeed to this prayer time, but more an outcome of a "being-becoming" vision of yourself. What you do is important. Who you are is more significant.

Centering prayer, like other forms of Christian meditation, should be a long-term commitment. Meditation is not a quick fix for spiritual growth. Look at a tree. Feel the toughness of its bark. Listen to how silently it grows. Count the years that brought it to this height and thickness. Admire the foliage, especially its autumn color. Ponder its wintry bareness. Rejoice with its spring green. It is an image of your personal spiritual development. The very first psalm in the Bible says that a happy, spiritual person is "like a tree planted near running water" (Psalm 1:3). Be content to let the years nourish your mystery.

Prayer

Jesus, my teacher, my spiritual master, lead me into the paths of meditation. You robed yourself in the silence of night when you meditated under the stars upon a mountain. Your personal presence, words and deeds were meditation starters, moments in which you awoke in others the sense of their mystery and their capacity for prayer. I know that even to look at you moves me to sense your inner vitality and makes me aware of my own. Hold me close to you and I shall begin to know myself—and you—more intimately.

Chapter Four

JESUS, MY LORD

The Son of God

I enjoy reading history. John Julius Norwich's spellbinding history of Constantinople so captivated me that I was moved to visit the sites of the first four general councils of the Church he described so vividly. In these stormy councils the bishops hammered out new understandings of the biblical teaching about the humanity and divinity of Jesus.

The Road to Nicaea

Permit me to begin this meditation on the divinity of Jesus with an account of my visit to Nicaea, where Christ's divinity was freshly affirmed in 325. I launched my pilgrimage from Istanbul (formerly Constantinople) by taking a two-and-a-half-hour voyage across the Sea of Marmora to Yalova. From there I would take an hour's bus ride to Iznik, the Turkish name for Nicaea, where the first council was held. I used the travel time to study photocopied pages about the history of the Council.

The fact that I was the only Christian on a ship

with a thousand Muslims was daunting. Midway through the trip, a university student sitting next to me noticed me studying and underlining the text. "Are you doing research?" he asked. "Yes," I replied. "Where are you going?" he asked. "To Nicaea," said I. "Oh, you mean Iznik. You must be a Christian." I told him I was. He explained that he was an engineering student and a devout Muslim. He asked me, "Tell me: How can Jesus be divine?" On the page I was reading was exactly the same question. Knowing he could speak English and assuming he could read it as well, I pointed to the question on the page and said, "You see, your ancestors were asking the same question sixteen hundred years ago." I also showed him another sentence in the text which said, "Those who try to answer this question must be out of their minds."

I explained that we believe in the divinity of Jesus because our faith tells us that God revealed this truth to us. It remains a mystery even though we try to find words to explain it. He listened attentively and thoughtfully when I went on to tell him how the Church Fathers interpreted the mystery in terms of one divine Person united to a human and divine nature in Jesus.

When we arrived at Yalova, he was kind enough to take me to the ticket booth, help me with the purchase, accompany me to the right bus and wait until I departed. He was the embodiment of Islamic courtesy, and I shall never forget him.

The road to Nicaea was flanked by mountains and olive groves on one side and the fifty-mile-long Lake Iznik on the other. I arrived at modern Nicaea, which still has a Roman wall around it, the remains of a Roman theater and the excavation of a Christian church built in the fourth century. A sign in front of the church announced that the Second Council of Nicaea was held there in the seventh century.

I took pictures of the restored church, prayed the Nicene Creed and reflected on the history of the First Council of Nicaea. A Lybian-born priest named Arius preached that Jesus was not really divine in the same sense that the one God was divine. He taught that God created a Logos, a Word by which the world was made. When the world needed salvation, the created Word took flesh in Jesus. To reward him for his fine work, God "adopted" Jesus as a minor divinity, to be esteemed more than other people. Arius dramatized his teachings in catchy popular songs, winning thousands of converts and enlisting many bishops to his cause.

Emperor Constantine I opposed this religious divisiveness. He had brought political unity to the Roman Empire. He argued there should only be one emperor, one empire, one religion, one God. He summoned a Church council at Nicaea to make sure that religion and God would not be divisive elements in his new empire. Bishops with the traditional faith in the full divinity of Jesus (not a "created and adopted" divinity) saw the council as an opportunity to counter Arius. Three hundred eighteen bishops attended the council (including Nicholas of Myra who would become St. Nicholas. Folk history would transform him into Santa Claus.).

Fierce debates ensued between the Arian bishops and theologians and the Catholic ones.

Eventually, the Catholic party prevailed, arguing that Jesus, the Word made flesh, was of the same divine nature as the Father.

It was not hard for me to imagine their lively sessions as I gazed on the town where it was held. Then I heard the afternoon Muslim call to faith in the one God. I added, "...in three persons, Father, Son and Spirit."

To speak of Jesus as my Lord is to affirm my faith in his divinity. This raises certain questions. How does the New Testament speak of Christ's divinity? Why did the Son of God become a human being? What difference does that make for me? I offer you here my responses to each of these questions.

The New Testament and Christ's Divinity

In a variety of ways, the New Testament tells us that Jesus is divine. In a debate with his followers, Jesus said, "[B]efore Abraham came to be, I AM" (John 8:58b). Thus, his existence did not start in Mary's womb. He was alive before that. By calling himself "I AM," he identified himself with the name of God given to Moses at the burning bush (see Exodus 3:14)—and therefore with God.

The author of the Letter to the Hebrews describes the Son of God as the Word. In the past, God had spoken to the world through the prophets. In his Son, Jesus, God speaks completely, expressing the fullness of divine revelation. This Son "is the refulgence of [God's] glory, the very imprint of his being" (Hebrews 1:3a). In effect, God can say, "In my

Word, I have said everything. Fix your eyes on Jesus alone. In him you will find more than you could ever ask for or desire."

John picks up this theme in the opening of his Gospel by telling us plainly:

> In the beginning was the Word,
> and the Word was with God
> and the Word was God....
> And the Word became flesh
> and made his dwelling among us,
> and we saw his glory,
> the glory as of the Father's only Son,
> full of grace and truth. (John 1:1, 14)

Paul affirms the divinity of Jesus:

> Who, though he was in the form of God,
> did not regard equality with God something to be grasped.
> Rather, he emptied himself,
> taking the form of a slave,
> coming in human likeness.... (Philippians 2:6-7a)

The eternal Word, born of the Father before time began, was born into this world as a human being, as the son of Mary. "When the fullness of time had come, God sent forth his Son, born of a woman..." (Galatians 4:4a).

In a powerful scene in John's Last Supper account, Jesus makes a unique connection between the Father and himself. He had been speaking so joyfully about the Father that Philip impetuously interrupted him and said, "Master, show us the Father, and that will be enough for us" (John 14:8b).

Philip and the others did not yet appreciate the full reality of Jesus. Despite his witness, teachings and miracles Jesus had not yet been able to awaken their awareness of his full identity. They had been the students of the most extraordinary spiritual tutorial in history but still needed to grasp the ultimate meaning of it all. They heard Jesus' magnificent sermons, saw his wondrous miracles, lived intimately on a most personal level with him, watched him in debates, listened to him solve problems, took miles of walks with him, lingered after dinner in conversation with him and felt the remarkable magnetism of his personality. Although Jesus had used every imaginable means to reach them and change them, it seems he had barely touched the surface of their minds and hearts.

Philip and the apostles had plenty of evidence about Jesus. They had sight, but they did not have insight. They had lots of data but no real meaning. They knew as much as any survey could ever tell them, yet missed the point of it all. They suffered from a very human folly that believes that externals reveal the true state of the internal life of another.

Jesus used this opportunity to unveil his divinity. "Whoever has seen me has seen the Father" (John 14:9b). Intimacy alone had not disclosed who he really was. He needed to give them an explicit revelation. While it was true that their incredible experience of him had not of itself led them to the final truth about his divinity, the encounters had prepared them for it. That is why he was willing to let lightning strike the Upper Room, a flash of revelation about his divinity.

Their knowledge of Scripture had taught them that one could not look on the face of God and live.

Moses bowed his eyes to the ground at the burning bush. He veiled his face when talking to God. Jesus revealed a new possibility to the apostles. They could look on the face of God and live. In fact they *should* do so, for by looking at the face of Jesus they would gain immeasurable insight into the reality of God. To see Jesus was to see the Father.

Jesus does not claim to *be* the Father, but the face, the icon of the Father in the world. Jesus is "the image of the invisible God" (Colossians 1:15b). In times past the vision of God struck fear and trembling into the hearts of the prophets. That holy night, in the friendly, reassuring glow of candlelight around the Passover table, in a mood of palpable affection, the apostles were privileged to look at God's face in the countenance of Jesus. They were not frightened. Because of Jesus, the Father is present at that table, perfectly united to his Son. Love prevailed at that banquet.

It would still take the death and resurrection of Jesus and the coming of the Holy Spirit at Pentecost to help them grasp this revelation and realize the scope of its truth. Ten days later, in that very same room, the doubting Thomas came to faith in Christ's divinity. In adoration he whispered, "My Lord and my God" (John 20:28b).

The New Testament says a great deal more about the divinity of Jesus. In the Book of Revelation, Jesus is frequently called the Lamb, and is the joyful focus of the angels' songs, just as he was when he was born at Bethlehem:

Worthy is the Lamb that was slain
    to receive power and riches, wisdom and strength,

honor and glory and blessing. (Revelation 5:12b)

Scripture gives us the basic response to Jesus, my Lord, both in the confession of Thomas and the hymns of the angels.

Why Did the Son of God Become Human?

The Son of God became a human being to liberate us from the power of sin and to fill us with divine love, a synonym for divine life. When we speak of Jesus as our savior, we describe him as a liberator *from* evil and a liberator *for* love. While Chapter Seven will deal with this truth in further detail, I will also reflect on it here with you, since it is so intimately related to his divinity.

Jesus, Liberator From Sin

Much of modern philosophy and the arts dwell on the state of current Western culture. Philosophers tell us about our alienation, our loss of meaning and purpose in life. The dissonances of contemporary classical music capture the dislocations of our souls. The primitive colors, the raging abstractions and the dismembered figures on our artists' canvases capture the torments of the modern soul. Stream-of-consciousness writers such as James Joyce confront us with the disconnectedness we experience in our heads.

These insightful thinkers and artists unsparingly hold our souls up to us for inspection. It is not a pretty sight. Sad to say, we have made a hell out of our lives on earth. Since 1914, with Auschwitz and Cambodia's killing fields as prime exhibits, war has made our time the bloodiest century in history. In *Three Philosophies of Life*, philosopher Peter Kreeft says that our present hell is uniquely our own and it is based on our fear:

> Modernity's greatest fear is not so much the fear of death (that was ancient man's deepest fear), or the fear of sin, guilt or Hell (that was medieval man's deepest fear), but the fear of meaninglessness, of "vanity," of the "existential vacuum," the fear of Nothingness.

When there is no purpose, there is meaninglessness, nothing, no-thing, nonbeing. When there is purpose to our lives, there is meaning, some-thing, being, some-One. Dislocated from God, we lose the map of life and plunge into destructive chaos.

The Bible teaches us that in the beginning there was chaos and God made a cosmos out of it. Along came humans and they threw the world back into chaos. The three images in the Book of Genesis 1—11 tell just such a story: The disobedience of Adam and Eve resulted in their expulsion from Eden into a life of suffering. The sinfulness of their descendants led to a return of the chaotic flood that nearly reversed creation altogether. The arrogance of the builders of Babel caused a chaos of tongues and a breakdown of meaning and communion.

Scripture teaches, however, that God is on the side of humanity, creation, purpose, meaning and hope. To Adam and Eve he promised a figure who would crush the head of the evil that lures us to self-destructive behavior. In the face of the destroying flood, God rescued Noah and his family by means of an ark. The rainbow after the flood indicated that God has no intention of abandoning his master plan for redeeming creation from chaos. In the aftermath of Babel, God called Abraham and began a relationship with the generations of people covenanted with him in faith.

God has not forgotten contemporary culture either. The words spoken to the Ephesians in the first century of Christianity are equally addressed to us today: "[H]e chose us in [Jesus], before the foundation of the world, to be holy and without blemish before him. In love he destined us for adoption to himself through Jesus Christ..." (Ephesians 1:4-5a). Jesus is a Son in the divine family. God wants you and me to be adopted daughters and sons—each a child of divine love—of the original Family: Father, Son and Spirit. We are to be "joint heirs with Christ" (Romans 8:17b).

God is the supreme rescuer of human beings from their own folly and sinfulness. Ephesians teaches us that there is a divine plan for the world, a purpose for history, a meaning centered in the saving work of Jesus. Divorced from God, we slide into self-made chaos. United with God in Jesus, we rise from our self-inflicted depression to a life of love, creativity, hope and true fulfillment. The Son of God became a human being to make that possible.

Original Sin

From the story of Adam's sin and its effects, Christian theology created the term "original sin" to describe the moral slavery which threatens the hopes of each of us. This condition is both social and personal. Our cultural environment, though it contains signs of hope, goodness and love, is unbalanced toward the side of destruction. Theology has long taught that the inner life of humans will evidence a drive—often overwhelming—to evil. Today's philosophers and artists are telling us the same thing. Yes, friends, original sin is alive and, regrettably, well.

Without a doubt, many people in our culture are fighting back, but often with tools that are not up to the battle. We place our hopes for redemption on education, prosperity, conversation, dialogue, relationship skills and positive thinking. All this is helpful, but it is not enough. It never gets to the root of the problem—which is spiritual sickness. Kierkegaard said it well a century ago: that we are succumbing to a "sickness unto death."

Therapists tell us that we cannot be healed of an emotional or mental illness unless we first admit we have a problem. This is just as true of spiritual illness. Until we admit our sinfulness, we cannot be saved from it. That is the first step. A second one is equally important: Until we believe that there is a higher power that can rescue us, we cannot be saved. That higher power is Jesus, the Son of the living God.

Why Paul Preached Only Jesus

When St. Paul went to Corinth, it was the "sin city" of his day. This prosperous city in southern Greece, with access to two harbors and situated in the middle of the Mediterranean shipping lanes, was the mecca for sailors, soldiers, merchants and civil servants from all over the empire. It was a pluralistic culture with widespread sexual freedoms. To live like a Corinthian was to espouse an "anything goes" philosophy. "Corinthian girl" meant a call girl. The adventurous males prayed to Aphrodite in the temple crowning the hill that overlooked the city for good luck in their lustful pursuits. One ancient account claims there were one thousand prostitutes available near the temple. There was lots to drink. One excavation unearthed a building that housed thirty-three taverns.

When he preached in Athens, Paul used a cultural approach. He cited poets and philosophers and included observations about Athenian art and sculpture (see Acts 17). He felt uneasy about the effectiveness of his mission strategy in Athens, even though he made some converts. But faced with the raw power of self-destructive sinfulness in Corinth, Paul decided he needed a more powerful and substantial message. Listen to his own words. When you hear him talk about human wisdom, recall that he is thinking of his Athenian experience.

> I did not come with sublimity of words or of wisdom. For I resolved to know nothing while I was with you except Jesus Christ, and him crucified.... [M]y message and my proclamation were not with persuasive [words of] wisdom, but with a demonstration of spirit and power, so that your faith might rest not on human wisdom but on the power of God. (1 Corinthians 2:1b-2; 4-5)

Paul clearly relied on Jesus to rescue the Corinthians from the power of sin. Why did the Son of God become a human being? First, to liberate us from the power of sin. Second, to give us divine love and life.

Jesus, Liberator for Love

Once Jesus delivers us from the oppression of evil, he unblocks our drive to self-transcendence, a process marked by the freedom that comes from love. We experience ourselves as part of God's intimate family. We walk confidently forward to our true destiny, our family home, experienced in loving relations here on earth and perfectly fulfilled when we go to heaven. Scripture describes this process of belonging to God's family in terms of our relation to the Holy Spirit. Jesus sends us his Spirit to lead us to love: "For those who are led by the Spirit of God are children of God. For you did not receive a spirit of slavery to fall back into fear, but you received a spirit of adoption, through which we cry, '*Abba*, Father!' " (Romans 8:14-15).

As members of the Lord's family we share in the gifts of the household. The Spirit, who is the embodiment of love, awakens within us seven powers of love that were dormant under the oppression of sin. The Spirit enables us to develop these powers and thus fulfill our calling to be daughters and sons of the family of God. What are these powers and what can they do for us?

1) Wisdom: This power relates to our judgment. It summons us to judge people and events from a perspective as deep and compassionate as God's own. Shakespeare was thinking of wisdom when he wrote the speech in *The Merchant of Venice* where Portia tells the judge about the need to temper justice with mercy. Wise people bring the warmth of loving compassion to their evaluation of human problems, weaknesses and dilemmas. Everyone is born with the potential to be wise. For those liberated by Jesus and led by the Spirit this potential for seeing people as God sees them is activated.

2) Understanding: This power concerns the quest for meaning. It certainly involves making sense out of life by using our minds and applying rules of logic. But that is only half the story, our calculating side. The Spirit invites us to develop the power we have to receive meaning, to let truth speak to us. Pascal meant this when he told us about the heart having reasons of which the mind does not know. Some people speak of this as intuitive ability associated with "right brain" thinking.

The Spirit calls us to move beyond just laboriously making sense out of life to relaxing a bit and letting life and God offer us meaning. How else can we expect to understand the meaning of religious truths? Both aspects of understanding are necessary— meaning-making and meaning-receiving, but it is the latter that we generally ignore. Making meaning is a mind game. Receiving meaning is an act of a lover listening to the beloved.

3) Knowledge: This power gives us confidence that we can know the truth. The communications revolution overwhelms us with facts. Did you know that the average supermarket contains thirty thousand items? The flood of information causes over-choice, and sometimes paralysis of choice. The sheer number of facts suggests that perhaps truth cannot be known. Truth is not the same as facts. Truth is a correct interpretation of facts. Truth is more than a subjective analysis of facts. It is an objective evaluation.

The Spirit touches our power for knowing truth and draws us to be convinced that it exists. Jesus claimed he taught truth and that, indeed, he was living truth. The Spirit invites us to daily loving union with Jesus, who communicates this conviction about truth. Because we are journeying in an environment of love, we cannot help but become truth-centered, for real lovers do not lie.

4) Counsel: Has history ever had so many counselors? Universities graduate thousands of them every year. If there were not a need for so much guidance, there would not be a market for it. In a confused world people need some light about what to do. Thank God there are so many willing to help.

But within our hearts is a power for guiding ourselves. It is called our conscience. In a sense, this is our internal counseling room, where our powers of knowledge, understanding and wisdom dialogue to help us make moral decisions.

We do more than talk to ourselves. We also have the inner light of the Spirit shedding divine illumination on our proceedings. We have a divine partner at the table of our conscience. Our counsel is a conviction that we can do what is creative, loving and productive for ourselves, others and God.

5) Courage: Some have said that courage is the best proof for God's existence. We sense the divine presence when we witness such acts of courage as a fireman rescuing a baby from a burning building.

Courage gives people the power to live what they profess. Why do the lives of Joan of Arc, Thomas More and Maximilian Kolbe inspire us? Their courageous willingness to die for what they believe speaks to our own potential for this kind of witness. As long as there are martyrs, there will be a Church. The blood of martyrs is always the seed of a fresh generation of believers.

Today our gift of courage has plenty of opportunities for expression. It takes courage for couples to work on their marriages in a nonsupportive environment. Legislators need courage to stick with their moral principles when campaigning and making laws. Professionals in medicine, science, business and schools require courage to resist dehumanizing and immoral philosophies. The Spirit drew forth so much courage from the original Christians that they evangelized the Roman empire. The same Spirit is here today.

6) Spirituality: Traditional religious language calls this power the gift of piety. The term *piety* has lost some of its ability to motivate us because of its association with hypocrisy and indifference to people's needs. That is why I choose to call it the power of spirituality. It directs attention to our interior attitudes, which should concentrate on Jesus and our ultimate destiny in God. The power of spirituality works best when we permit ourselves to be led by the Holy Spirit.

The Gospels often portray the influence of the Spirit in the life of Jesus. If Jesus allowed himself to be led by the Spirit, then we should be eager to do the same. We can tell this is happening to us when we make the spiritual goals of faith, hope and love the priorities of our lives. We will be sure of it when Jesus is our center.

7) *Fear of the Lord:* There is bad fear and good fear. I wrote of unpromising fear of failure, rejection, pain and death in Chapter Two. We should let go of this fear. But there is good fear as well. This is the caution we exercise when crossing a busy street, our watchfulness for muggers in a dangerous neighborhood, the protective care we provide for our children. On the spiritual level, good fear guards us from self-destroying attraction to evil. Good fear also induces reverence for God. This does not refer to the groveling of a slave, but to a sense of place, a modesty that honestly acknowledges the remarkableness of God. If we tremble like the angels before God, we shiver with happiness in the face of so much beauty and love.

The Son of God became human to liberate us for love. To achieve this, he offers us his Holy Spirit, the very embodiment of love. The Spirit activates in us the seven powers implanted in our souls. If we let ourselves be led by the Spirit, we will transcend ourselves through these seven ways of loving—and discover immense happiness in the bargain.

What Difference Does Christ's Divinity Make?

Today we tend to think mostly of the human Jesus. In an age which has seen so much dehumanization, we rightly struggle to reaffirm human dignity. Moreover, the more we examine our humanity the more impressed we become with its extraordinary mystery. Psychology and modern philosophy have caused us to be as intrigued by our inner space as by outer space. Psychology involves us with the wonders and terrors, the neuroses and possibilities of our psyches. Philosophy asks us to notice our drive to question, to quest and transcend ourselves.

This moves us to explore our religion from "below" rather than from "above." Or perhaps I should say from "within" rather than "without." We prefer to begin our religious quest by a journey into our inner selves. This is why we like to center on the human Jesus as the model for human inwardness, human dignity and the example of how to behave in a life-affirming manner.

Vatican II captured this approach with these words, "...Christ the Lord, Christ the new Adam, in the very revelation of the mystery of the Father and his love, fully reveals us to ourselves and brings to light our most high calling" (*The Church in the Modern World*, #22). The sentence includes Jesus as divine (the Lord) and human (new Adam). It is because of his divinity that he is able to reveal the mystery of the Father and his love. It is because of his humanity that he can show us how we can fully understand ourselves and our fullest potential ("our most high calling").

Psychology and philosophy tell us a great deal about ourselves. For that we should be properly appreciative. However, the Council Fathers teach us that only Jesus can fully reveal who we are and what we are ultimately called to be. The more we explore our inner lives, the more we will sense our own mystery. The more we linger by the humanity of Jesus, the more we will be drawn into his extraordinary mystery—his divinity. His humanity is like the door to a Gothic cathedral. The door may be twenty feet high and several feet wide. Inside we behold breathtaking height, grandeur, color and the urge to soar. We experience a divine presence.

His divinity makes a difference to us because through it he links our human development to our divine destiny. His divinity makes a difference because it provided the power of liberation from sin and liberation for love which the Son of God exercised through his humanity. We learn that we are fully human when we transcend ourselves, with the Spirit's guidance and gifts, by living a divine life with divine love.

Trapped in sin, we can only devolve to a state that is less than human. When the roadblock of sin is removed by the divine power of Jesus, we enter a state of becoming who we were meant to be according to the divine plan. Sin causes us to be static and deteriorating. When Jesus liberates us, we become dynamic and growing. That is why his divinity, which causes this, makes a difference.

Reflection

The mystery of the divinity of Jesus, my Lord, has been explained in various ways. We read about it in the New Testament, in the words of Nicaea, the teachings of Aquinas and contemporary writers such as Karl Rahner and Hans Urs Von Balthasar. We hear it sung about every Christmas in lovely carols. We have lots of words. We are properly aware that we should never ignore the humanity *or* the divinity of Jesus. I suggest we also need some silence to hear Jesus himself speak directly to our hearts about his inner mystery.

The following exercises are directed to this purpose. I developed these exercises after reading "God's Two Silences," in John Main's book, *The Way of Unknowing* (Crossroad, New York, 1990).

The Silence of the Presence of Jesus

1) Find a quiet place and plan to relax in silence for at least twenty minutes.

2) Choose a comfortable position.

3) Induce a sense of silence by practicing breath-counting for several minutes. Notice your natural inhaling. As you begin to exhale, quietly say to yourself, "One." Do this until you get to four. Then start over. Do not attempt to breathe more deeply. Just let your body do what comes naturally. If you go beyond four, or forget what number you are on, go back to one. When you have done this for a while, and feel relaxed, go to the next step.

4) Visualize Jesus alone, gazing into a campfire. Hear his words, "I am the light of the world" (John 8:12b).

5) Quietly say these words and pause. Say them slowly, allowing silence between each word: "I...am...the...light...of...the...world."

6) Allow his presence to affect you in your silence.

7) Use the saying to restore your focus when you seem to be drifting toward outer concerns.

8) Do nothing else but this.

9) After twenty minutes thank Jesus for the experience with the words, "Jesus my light, my Lord, I love you."

The Silence of the Absence of Jesus

1) Select a quiet place. Choose a comfortable position. Plan to be silent for twenty minutes.

2) Settle down with the breath-counting exercise described above.

3) You will not need to focus on Christ's absence. You will find that after a certain number of meditation experiences, you will cease, from time to time, to sense the presence of Jesus. Your resolve to stay with the exercise is a sign of maturing, your willingness to rest in Jesus even when you are not feeling the warmth of his presence. In doing this you "lose your self" and the need to have such spiritual pleasure. Love alone is enough for you.

4) Visualize the Last Supper. Hear Jesus say to Philip, "Whoever has seen me has seen the Father" (John 14:9b). Rest in your silence for twenty minutes. Use these words to lead you back to your center whenever you find yourself returning to your daily preoccupations.

5) If Jesus seems to be absent from your experience,

do not panic or be discouraged. Let love keep you attentive. Absence deepens your longing for Jesus.

6) Close with this prayer:

> Jesus, my Lord, I praise you and long for you. I thirst for your presence. Save me from my sins. Liberate me for love. Give me your Spirit to increase my capacity for wisdom, knowledge, understanding, counsel, courage, spirituality and fear of the Lord. I walk in a little bit of darkness. I wish to be led by your Spirit into the abundance of your light, which actually surrounds me. I choose the silence. I adore you and give you my will.

Chapter Five

JESUS, MY MENTOR

The Three Stages of Discipleship

When I was a professor at Catholic University in
Washington, D.C., I was asked by the department
chairman to teach a two-semester course in Judeo-
Christian studies to the non-Catholic students. Since
all undergraduates were required to take four
semesters of religion courses, the department offered
alternatives for those who were not Catholic. One of
these was the class to which I was assigned.

My students were mostly Protestants and Jews, a
few from Asian religions and one ex-Communist
seaman, named Ivan, who had jumped ship in
Liverpool and defected the year before. I chose the
Bible as the core text for the courses. I drew on ideas
from a variety of Jewish, Protestant and Catholic
writers.

I told my students that they were responsible for
the academic material in any exam, which often
meant reporting various religions' interpretations of
the Bible. Though I did not test them on their
personal beliefs, I urged them to be active
practitioners of their faiths. I made it clear when I was
talking as a Catholic and when I was attempting to

represent other faith views as fairly as I could. I invited their participation, objections and explanations of their own points of view. It was a yeasty mix, and we had many lively discussions and debates.

I recall that Ivan, fresh from his first-ever reading of the Bible, raised his hand and said, "Now I know why God does not like the Jewish people." He was drawing an anti-Semitic conclusion from his study, an attitude it turned out that he had brought with him from Russia. Needless to say, the other students landed on him, and I took time then and after class to disabuse him of his wrong interpretation and prejudice. I felt I was as much a mentor as a teacher in these classes.

I was able to dispel the prejudice even further by sharing with the students the meditative, spiritual teachings of Rabbi Abraham Joshua Heschel. Raised in the Hasidic mystical tradition in Poland, Heschel obtained a doctorate at the University of Berlin. He and his family emigrated to the United States when Hitler came to power. He became an outspoken supporter of the civil rights movement and a peace activist. His numerous books dwelt on the human search for God and God's quest for unity with people. He expressed himself in a prayerful, poetic and mystical style.

Three years later when I came to write my doctoral dissertation, I chose the writings of Heschel for my topic and showed how his insights were valuable for the teaching of religion. Soon after the completion of my doctorate, I was on an interfaith panel with Rabbi Marc Tannebaum and Rabbi Wolf

Kelman. I mentioned to them that I had written on Heschel and that I heard he was their teacher. Tannebaum replied, "He was not our teacher. He was our Master. We were his disciples." In other words, Heschel was their *mentor*. Having visited with Heschel several times, I could verify what they meant. His spiritual depth invited just such a relationship.

Their description of a "master-disciple" relationship reminded me of the Gospel portrayal of how Jesus and the apostles related to each other. A teacher imparts knowledge; a mentor shares wisdom. A teacher talks to the head; a mentor confronts the person. A teacher shapes a mind; a mentor influences a life. A teacher seeks agreement on ideas; a mentor desires commitment. A mentor expects disciples.

Jesus was indeed a teacher. He taught truth, meditation and a way of life. But he was also a mentor. He asked for commitment. He told his listeners that he was the way, the path to salvation and happiness. He outlined the principles for being his disciple. "Lose yourself. Take your cross. Follow me" (see Matthew 16:24). Before ascending to heaven, Jesus commissioned the apostles to become mentors themselves. He wanted them to make disciples just as he did. They were to do more than teach his ideas. They should persuade people to "do what he had commanded" (see Matthew 28:19-20). Learning his ideas was insufficient. Jesus expected discipleship.

The first step in discipleship is the loss of self. This has always been a difficult challenge for any follower of Jesus. Today it seems even more out of the question in a culture that insists on me-first individualism. A self-stroking society will be deaf to the call to lose the self.

But there is another more positive view of self which tells us that we need to build up our self-worth and have a healthy self-image. Virtually all therapy for drug, alcohol and other kinds of addictions teaches that a poor self-image is at the root of the problem. The negative self-image often results from childhood trauma or is learned from parents who have the same problem. Social oppressions such as dehumanizing poverty and prejudice are also contributing causes. How can we expect such people to lose their "selves" that are already in such a state of disrepair?

I would answer that Christ's call remains applicable. Persons with low self-esteem must go through an extra stage—a therapeutic one where they trade the poor self-image for a healthy one. Then they can enter the spiritual stage and lose the stabilized self-image to acquire an even better one in Christ. Without the therapeutic stage, they have such a frail sense of self that there is no real self to lose. It is the restored self that needs the rebirth of which Jesus spoke.

So I grant in advance the need for the first step where necessary and cede that development to the competent hands of therapists. Indeed, such a process is part of God's providential care, healing people and preparing them for a deeper journey. Here I wish only to speak of the loss of self in those who have a self to lose.

The issue is complex, and there is no one infallible way to do it. This is because the human person is such a mystery. A lot can be known, but there is so much more to say. I can ask you to tell me the story of Tolstoy's *War and Peace* in fifty words or less. You might give me some general story lines, but you will necessarily leave out over a thousand pages of narrative. The human mystery is something like this: Much will be revealed only through time and experience.

It is common enough to use models to unravel the fascinating mystery of a person. Remembering that a model is just a useful tool, not the last word on the subject, I offer a model to describe how the self can be lost and a better self gained. My model is derived from the common-sense observation that there is a false self and a real self.

The central character in Susan Howatch's novel *Glittering Images* is a troubled Anglican priest whose spiritual stumbling block is his attachment to his glittering image, his false self. Howatch outlines the process of his redemption through dramatic encounters with a spiritual mentor who roughly and gently walks with him to the light of a true self and then to a self that permits Jesus to occupy the center of his life. Fulton J. Sheen uses a similar paradigm in his 1955 book *Lift Up Your Heart*. Loss of self demands the shedding of the false self to find the real self, and eventually to surrender the real self to Jesus.

'Leggo Your Ego'

The first step is to lose your false self, which I will call your ego. The real you is your "I." Imagine a circle in which a screaming ego commands the middle ground. The "I" is in a penalty box on the margin of the circle. The ego is in control. The ego maintains its domination by following these five maxims:

The Ego Obeys the Culture

Having no inner resources of its own, the ego feeds on the culture. It is bonded to the spirit of the times and takes its cue from what others command. The ego does not know that one who marries the spirit of the times soon becomes widowed. Allied to this servitude is the ego's preoccupation with the body. Looking good means a lot—too much, in fact. Slavery to the body turns the ego into an actor who is always polishing the surfaces of the body, reshaping it to fit whatever the arbiters of culture tell it is acceptable. The body serves as the expression of the ego's communion with the culture.

In old-fashioned terms, the result is vanity, emptiness, the sudden wilting of the rose and the frantic desire to rescue what can only decay. Anxiety eats at the ego. Jesus noticed this and appealed to people to lose such fears about eating and fashion. God's eye is on the sparrow and the flowers of the field (see Matthew 7:25-34). Peace of heart begins with trust in God, not the ego's childish obedience to the culture. Only the true self is capable of such trust.

The Ego Uses Emotion to Make Decisions

The ego can deal only with the physical and the sensate. It can only handle what is seen, touched and felt. The life of the mind and the force of the spirit scare the ego because they will seize control from it and spoil the party. Hence the ego chooses the feelings as the source of judging what should be done. If it hears the voice of conscience, it sings, "It can't be bad if it feels so good." Morality is a matter of emotion. Truth is whatever feels OK.

The result is a chaotic life in which the quest for happiness is crying for louder music and madder love. Governed by passions and feelings, the ego sails through ever more turbulent waters in a tragic parody of the journey of the real self. The captain of the ship is the most unsteady of all human faculties, the emotions. Jesus described this as building a house on sand (see Matthew 7:24-27). The winds blow and the waves roll in and sweep the ego-house away. Only the house of the "I," which is built on the rock of principles, logic and faith will endure.

The Ego Uses People and Loves Things

A beautiful young farm woman once placed a personal ad in a magazine. "Blond woman, 25, healthy and attractive, owner of a new tractor, seeks compatible male. Picture available." The first letter she received said, "Send picture of tractor."

Since the ego has no spiritual power, it can only use people to stroke its needs. The ego is the original con artist. Because it is unable to love people, the ego can only destroy them. It consumes people to feed its life; it is a parasite on society. Like evil, the ego has no life of its own, but lives only by chewing up the good that it finds. This is why extramarital affairs, casual trysts and other forms of uncommitted arrangements die so quickly. The partners suck the life out of each other, take whatever human sweetness is there and then dispose of one another like an empty milk carton.

The ego is incapable of love because it has no spiritual content. Only the "I" can love and be loved. That is why Jesus makes love the greatest of his commandments. Jesus speaks to the center of love in each person, the "I," and invites the "I" to do what comes naturally. The real self will love people and use things. The real self is not a parasite consuming lives. The real self is a bountiful giver of affection and creative love.

The Ego Loves Only the Feeling of Love

The ego always uses the language of love, but it only likes the warmth of love, not its demands or sacrifices. It takes the pleasure and runs away from the responsibility. It prefers the thrill, not the commitment. It likes the chase but dreads the capture. The ego is a living greeting card: full of sweet sentiments, smelling of perfume, scrolled with touching feelings. But no person comes with the card, just a shadow as insubstantial as a cloud. The ego is a creature of compromise, a champion of short-term involvement, a lover of sugar that does not believe in suffering for a loved one or dying for what one believes.

Jesus understands that we need the pleasurable experience of love. He gave the Emmaus disciples the "burning hearts" experience that flooded them with loving feelings. But he did that while he told them why the Son of Man had to suffer and die for love and enter into glory (see Luke 24:13-35). Their experience occurred in a context of deep interpersonal communion and a challenge to heroic sacrifice. The ego could never do that. But the "I" can and should.

The Ego Hides the "I"

When the ego isn't busy identifying with the culture, it expends considerable energy in repressing the true self. The ego knows it must marginalize the real self if it is going to survive. It imprisons the "I" in the penalty box of the soul. It rightly fears the thunderous resources of the mind, the will and the spirit which threaten its playtime, its very existence. The ego, after all, is a lie, not the true self. It consumes a person's energy capital to maintain its sway of bread and circuses. It weakens the will, blinds the mind and chokes the spirit with the energy spent on the pursuit of the pleasures of the flesh and the world.

Jesus remorselessly replies, "Kill your ego and liberate your 'I.' " Lose the false self to find the real one. On the eve of his passion, Jesus met with some Greeks who had asked to see him (see John 12:20-26). We do not know what they said. We know Christ's answer, but we are not given the question. Allow me to speculate a moment on what the Greeks might have proposed to him.

They may have reminded him of the story of Socrates, sentenced to drink poisonous hemlock by the unaccepting Athenians. Ever since, the wise people of Athens had regretted pushing so great a philosopher to his death. The Greek pilgrims in

Jerusalem had heard of the extraordinary wisdom of Jesus, as well as rumors about death threats. Perhaps they communicated their anxious concern for his safety to Jesus. Possibly they tried to persuade him to emigrate to Athens, where he would find a congenial and nonthreatening audience, where he would be honored as a mentor and wise man. The world capital of philosophy would appreciate and love him.

Perhaps that was their proposal. Surely it would have been a seductive offer, a reasonable alternative to the murderous danger that confronted Jesus. If so, then his reply seems even more powerful.

"...[U]nless a grain of wheat falls to the ground and dies, it remains just a grain of wheat; but if it dies, it produces much fruit" (John 12:24b, c). This is Jesus, my mentor, speaking. He is more interested in bearing witness as a mentor than in being an honored philosopher. He had preached the loss of self. He would now show the full extent of what he meant. His message was an essential truth; his redemptive death would be its lived fulfillment.

The only way out of the deadly grip of the ego is to die to it. It is better to be bonded to Jesus than to the culture. A wholesome Christian life puts the emotions at the service of the mind and the will. The real self will love persons and put things in perspective. The "I" will embrace responsibility and commitment whether there is a romantic thrill in the encounter or not. Kill the ego; let the "I" out of the penalty box; grow up. That will occur when the ego falls to the ground and dies. The resurrection of the real self replaces it.

The process of losing the self is not over. The second stage begins. Now imagine a new circle: Behold the "I" gloriously reigning in the center of the field. See the ego whimpering in the penalty box on the margin. Remember that it never completely goes away. The ego sticks around, nibbling at the edges of our goodness for its daily maintenance. St. Paul spoke of it as a thorn in his side that he wished God would remove (see 2 Corinthians 12:7-9). Part of the responsibility of the real self is the daily struggle to kill off the false one. God has given us sufficient grace to make that possible.

What, then, guides the life of the true self?

A Love-Hate Relationship With the Culture

Our culture is like money. You can't live with it, and you can't live without it. Our relationship with it is bound to be ambiguous because one side of the culture favors human dignity and another side debases it. It is the task of the real self to discern the difference and act accordingly. The "I" should hate and fight against what threatens its integrity. The "I" should also love and nurture the positive elements of the culture, those that enhance the values that make life worth living. The "I" is simultaneously pro-culture and countercultural.

Jesus celebrated the life-affirming aspects of his culture. He gazed lovingly on the charm of village weddings, hummed along with the grape harvesters, swayed to the rhythm of harvest dances, enjoyed the beauty of the lilies of the fields, thrilled at an abundant catch of fish, took pleasure in sailing on Galilee and was a studious observer of religious practice and temple attendance. He wove many of these experiences into his teachings about happiness and life in the Kingdom.

Jesus also confronted the life-denying elements of his culture. He spoke against divorce, unmerciful business managers, adults who refused to support their parents, people obsessively concerned with food and clothing, the hypocrisy of religious leaders who emphasized the letter of the law while ignoring its spirit. By eating with sinners, fraternizing with lepers and the poor and standing with the culture's outcasts, Jesus took a countercultural stance. His "I" had a love-hate relationship with culture. So should ours.

Believing That the Truth Can Be Known

The ego never knows the truth because it uses emotions as the sole source of judgment. The "I" is more confident about knowing truth because it lives in the company of the intellect, the will and the spirit, God-given tools for apprehending truth. The "I" is well aware that this is always a process and sometimes a painful struggle. It will never be a dogmatist who thinks it knows all the answers. Neither will it be a skeptic who claims there are no answers.

The real self is committed to the search for truth because it is the foundation for becoming a good person. The ego wants to *feel* good; the "I" wants to *be* good. The principal reason for becoming a good person is that it is the only way to be truly happy. Evil gives the temporary illusion of happiness and leads a person to despair. Goodness, the fruit of truth's guidance, provides real joy and leads a person to hope.

Jesus said a great deal about truth because he came to make us happy, and truth is the only path to the goodness that makes joy possible. Truth is the map that shows the road to goodness, which is the source of happiness. That is why Jesus also claimed to *be* the truth: because he is the living road map of goodness and the author of real happiness. Hence the "I" will be a disciple of Jesus as mentor of truth.

Strengthening Your Willpower

The mind searches for answers and is confident that true ones can be found. The will is the drive to goodness based on the truth revealed by the mind. Thomas Aquinas spoke of the truths in the mind as "intellectual virtues." He meant that the mind not only can apprehend truth but also has a responsibility to think truthfully. Truth is more than correct ideas; it is a habit of thinking correctly. Otherwise true ideas become as disposable as the morning newspaper.

Aquinas also taught the necessity of practicing the moral virtues: prudence, justice, restraint and courage. Tradition calls them cardinal or "hinge" virtues because goodness and happiness are hinged, connected to their practice. In this view the unhinged person will be unhappy. It is the hinged-virtuous one who knows goodness and happiness.

Practicing the moral virtues is the responsibility

of willpower, which is guided by a truth-thinking mind. The purpose of this cooperative enterprise is a good life, which alone produces happiness. I should say here that this happiness is not without pain, suffering and disappointment. The achievement of goodness will entail pain. The mystery of suffering endures even when a good life is experienced, as is evident in the lives of Jesus, the saints and history's roll call of Christian witnesses. Paradoxically, happiness coexists with this pain—not perfect joy, for that is only possible in heaven, but a measure of joy that cannot be known in any other way in this life.

Willpower is needed to make the moral virtues effective forms of action in our lives. Willpower is the coach that calls us to repeat and repeat these hinge acts until they become second nature to us, sources of moral strength. Hence the "I" moves to goodness and happiness by seeking truth in the mind that justifies the efforts of willpower in the acquisition of the moral virtues.

I do not speak here of Pelagianism, which teaches that we do this by ourselves. I come from the Christian perspective, which asserts the need for Christ's grace and love, the Spirit's power and influence to take us every step of the way. We make this difficult moral journey with Jesus, our mentor, in the power of the Spirit. This is a joint venture between ourselves and our God. This is a cooperative enterprise in which divine love activates our drive to transcend ourselves. The "I" is always cooperating with divine love for this progress.

Nourishing Awareness of Personal Mystery

The "I" is always tempted to quantify itself. It may like to make lists of its good works and swell vainly, like a rooster crowing its presence to the world. The corrective is repeated attention to the mystery of the human person. The more the real self stays aware of its mystery, the more it will also appreciate the mystery of Jesus and the role of divine love in its life. How is this to be done? By meditation, reverence for people and a cultivated sense of wonder.

We have already looked at meditation and recommendations for centering prayer. The faithful practice of meditation will make us feel at home with our personal mystery.

We also foster an awareness of mystery by reverencing each person we meet. One way to do this is to recall the immortality of that person. All else will die and perish, but the human person will not. Human death is but a transition to a permanent life hereafter, either in heaven or hell. Whatever the outcome, the person is the most durable of all created realities. The more we are aware of this, the more we feel a sense of awe in meeting another human being.

Finally, if we cultivate a habit of wonder we will maintain a consciousness of the mystery of persons as well as all creation. As children we had a natural sense of wonder, which we tended to lose as we grew. As adults we again acquire a fresh capacity for wonder. That is why we have poets to reactivate our imagination, our inborn faculty for wonder. Wonder teaches us to look beyond the prosaic facts of life to the mystery that lies behind it all. The ability to wonder is similar to the capacity for the faith that affirms Christ's love behind all we perceive. Wonder is faith's valet. The divine poetry of the psalms is a workbook for growing in faith-filled wonder.

At the end of the second stage of our journey with Jesus, our mentor, we have become his disciples by losing the false self of our ego and acquiring the true self of the "I." One final stage is needed. The clue is found in St. Paul's statement, "...I live, no longer I, but Christ lives in me..." (Galatians 2:20a). In other words we must lose not only the false self; we must lose even our true self. The "not-I" must take over.

Surrender the Real You to Jesus

Biblical and spiritual literature often uses mountain-climbing images to describe the journey of faith. St. Benedict advises us how to climb the twelve rungs of the ladder of humility. John of the Cross guides us in the ascent of Mount Carmel. In these days of depth psychology we might benefit from thinking of the adventure as a descent instead of an ascent. Perhaps the Grand Canyon should be our master metaphor.

The safe plateau at the edge of the canyon is the watering hole of the ego. The risky plunge into the downward trails is the natural habitat of the "I." The willingness to go all the way to the mysterious center of the canyon brings us to the environment of the "not-I." Symbolically, we come to the nourishing womb of the earth. This is an image of the journey into our inner selves.

We have imagined two circles up to this point. In

the first one the ego commanded the center. In the second one the "I" took control. Now imagine a third circle in which Jesus holds the center ground. The "I" is in a penalty box at the edge, right next to a smaller box restraining the irrepressible ego, which is still gnawing at our sense of goodness and hoping for a comeback. Our scriptural teachings in this third stage come from John the Baptist, who said that Jesus must increase and he must decrease, and from Paul, who frankly tells us that Jesus alone is the driving force of his life.

The space between stages two and three must not be imagined too literally. By our imitation of Jesus in stage two we are already beginning to edge the "I" out of its prominent position. The diminishment of the "I" to make room for the ascendancy of Jesus is a slow and imperceptible process, much like the dying of a seed in the ground and the emergence of a stalk of wheat. The third stage is the maturing of the process. Here are two guiding principles for this stage:

Accept Your Cross

Buddha's first principle for living is to admit that life is hard, a matter of suffering. Buddha's teaching is a sound dose of realism, but its effect is a journey to a passive nirvana. There is a better way. Jesus equally tells us to stop our denial of suffering and death. The effect, however, is a dynamic participation with him in the salvation of people from all that oppresses them, above all from sin. When we reach this third stage of our journey and let Jesus move to the center, we will be more ready to surrender to his call to carry the cross prepared for us. We can do no other, for that is what Jesus himself did.

As we carry our cross in him and he in us, we begin to see the answers to evil, suffering and sin. We no longer deal with abstract ideas about solutions to these problems. We experience the answer in our union with a person, our mentor Jesus, the Son of God and the son of Mary. The response to our existential anxiety is an existential person. We have begged God for an answer to our troubles. His reply is the Word that is his Son. We will only know what the Word is saying when we walk with him on the road of the cross.

We realize that God took on suffering and pain through the Son, Jesus. Experientially, we discover how the cross of Jesus liberates us from sin, which ultimately is at the root of human suffering and death. Lastly, we peer through the pain to see that resurrection from our sin brings us resurrection from death. The cross is the final solution to these intractable problems. The "I" alone cannot reveal this to us. Only the "not-I" that is Jesus makes it plain.

Let Love Conquer All

The ego flounders because it mistakenly believes emotions alone can be the final guide to good behavior and happiness. The "I" can be tempted to believe that knowing abstract truths guarantees goodness and happiness. This would cause a separation between the intellectual and moral virtues. Thinking good thoughts becomes the substitute for proper behavior. In stage two this temptation is overcome by the practice of the moral virtues based upon thinking rightly.

Stage three brings Jesus to the command and control center of our selves. In him thought and love are fused into a unity in which love becomes the principle of action. Jesus is love, for God is love. This love is redeeming, liberating and creative. What does this cause in us? We see life as Jesus does. His thoughts become our thoughts. We love as he does, because we love with his love.

This sounds like a surrender of our independence, a loss of what makes me really me. In fact the opposite is true. I have at last become what I was called to be. Can anyone ever doubt the individuality of Paul or Catherine of Siena or Thomas More or Mother Teresa? They are very different people—all drenched with Jesus at the command and control center, yet so unique that they are unrepeatable individuals. Jesus never drowns the tender reed. In him we think as we were destined to think. In him we love as we were created to love. This is always accomplished in the total, memorable and special personhood we possess in a particular historical and cultural setting. It demands the three stages of discipleship: Leggo your ego. Welcome the real you. Surrender the real you to Jesus. We receive this gift of discipleship from Jesus, our mentor, when we obey his first command: Lose the self.

Reflection

There are many correct paths to discipleship. The model given here is a useful one, but not the only one. If it appeals to you, the following exercises will help you walk this road.

'Leggo Your Ego'

Is the culture controlling my life-style? If so, how could I change myself?

What kind of a role did emotion play in the last five important decisions I made? What do I need for rational decision-making?

Am I skilled at manipulating people? Am I a slave to shopping for things I don't need? What strategies could I adopt to treat people as persons and put things in a secondary place?

Do I want an experience of love without love's responsibility? What three steps could I take to overcome this?

Am I swept along by fashion and public opinion? What could I do to put my "I" in the command and control center of my consciousness?

Why is it important to listen to Jesus, my mentor, who tells me to let go of my ego-self?

Welcome the Real You

List five self-destructive aspects of modern society that should be fought against.

List five creative currents in the culture that deserve personal support and involvement.

Do I believe I can know the truth? Or do I think I can only know opinions that will change as circumstances change? If my answer is yes to the second question, how do I stay committed to Jesus, who claimed both to teach truth and to be the living truth?

Am I a weak-willed person? How could I chart the four hinge virtues of prudence, justice, restraint and courage for a daily exercise of these habits of the will?

If I acquire independence from obedience to my culture, achieve a mindset that is confident of knowing truth, and if my willpower is growing in moral virtue, am I doing this all by myself? Why would Jesus want me to lose my "I"?

Surrender the Real You to Jesus

When I examine my life, its joys and frustrations, its hopes and sufferings, what appears to be my real cross?

Am I more likely to run away from my cross or carry it? What kind of a daily spiritual program could I adopt that would help me to carry my cross with faith and in partnership with Jesus?

Why does it make sense in faith to lose my "I" and let Jesus be the driving force of my life?

If I compare my thoughts with those of Jesus, how similar are they?

Write down five acts of affection performed in the last week. Ask: How do my acts of love mirror the way Jesus would love? How do I become more Christ-like in my loving?

Prayer

Jesus, my mentor, you ask me to let go of my ego, welcome my real self to the center of my life and, finally, to let you be the driving force of my existence. Invite me hourly into the deep zone of silence within me. Bring me to the Holy Spirit, who waits there to teach me how to go through these three steps of discipleship. Hold me there until I permit the Spirit to assure me this is possible by the power of divine love. Keep after me. Shout to my deafness until I hear you. O Mentor, grant that I may seek to be no one else's disciple but yours.

Chapter Six

JESUS, MY SERVANT LEADER

The Social Gospel

Midway through my seminary years, I went to New York City to visit The Catholic Worker House. That August day was heavy with heat and humidity. The oppressive temperature made that shabby tenement building uninviting. Yet it was there that I met Dorothy Day. She and her coworkers were just finishing novena prayers, imploring God for the rent they needed for that month.

It also happened to be her birthday. They had a bottle of wine from which they doled out tiny portions to toast her. In the middle of their poverty they were rich with hospitality. I have no memory of what passed between me and Dorothy Day, just a lasting impression of her moral strength and her love of the poor.

One of her coworkers showed me around and pointed out that they lived as the poor lived, begging food and clothing for others and living from day to day on the providence of God. I was invited to supper in the soup kitchen. I recall seeing an old woman putting some extra bread into her purse. I had been raised in a poor family during the Depression, so I knew something of what these people were going through. It was abundantly clear to me that Dorothy Day and her disciples drew their motivation and energy from their spirituality. They took the command of Jesus to serve the poor very seriously and found in Christ the vision and power to carry out this mission.

My visit to The Catholic Worker House was a blessing and a grace that opened me to the Church's teaching on social justice and Christ's call to social ministry. The witness and instruction of Jesus is clear on this matter.

Jesus the Servant

After his temptations in the desert, Jesus began his public ministry. His inaugural address in the synagogue at Nazareth was a powerful statement on the need for justice and concern for the poor (see Luke 4:16-21).

The synagogue where he preached was as plain and unadorned as a village Congregational church in New England is today. The listeners sat on benches around a little platform on which was a chair and a reading stand. The service began with an opening prayer, followed by a reading from Scripture, a sermon and a discussion. The synagogue administrator supervised the proceedings.

After the prayer, the administrator gave Jesus a scroll on which was written the sixty-first chapter of Isaiah. Jesus chanted the words in Hebrew and followed it with a spoken translation in Aramaic, the dialect with which his listeners were more at home.

Then he rolled up the scroll, returned it to the administrator and sat down to give his sermon.

The words Jesus had read were about the "servant of the Lord," a saintly figure in Isaiah. The text mentioned that God's Spirit had come upon the servant. God sent the servant to bring good news to the lowly, to heal broken hearts, to announce freedom for those in prison and liberation for those suffering oppression. These words were traditionally interpreted as descriptions of what the Messiah would do when he came. Jesus' listeners surely loved this passage, which so well captured their desire for the Messiah and their hopes for freedom from Roman oppression.

Jesus was well aware of the political meaning his hearers associated with the reading. Some of them had relatives in prison for their opposition to the government. Rebellion was in the air. The sermons of John the Baptist convinced them that the Messiah was near. It was natural for them to link his coming with their willingness to mount a political and military revolt against Rome.

Jesus paused and let the silence attract their attention. "The eyes of all in the synagogue looked intently at him. He said to them, 'Today this scripture passage is fulfilled in your hearing'" (Luke 4:20b-21). It was an unexpected interpretation. Jesus was claiming that they were looking at the servant spoken of in the text—at the Messiah, that the Spirit had anointed him to fulfill the ministry described in Isaiah.

Much as they wanted a Messiah, they could scarcely believe it was Jesus, who had lived among them for thirty years and given no evidence that he could be such a person. It was the "prophet without honor" syndrome: Familiarity bred incomprehension.

Besides, Jesus was preaching a message much too spiritual for them: God's kingdom would produce liberation from oppression by the spiritual means of love, justice and mercy, not by armed revolt. He was not preaching political religion, but a faith that trusted in soul force, the moral power of character and personal witness. He was advocating social change that results from personal conversion, not from physical compulsion. They agreed with his goals, but they rejected his means. So deeply did they resent his nerve in identifying himself with the Messiah and his proposal to change the social order by peaceful means, that they drove him out of the synagogue and threatened to kill him (see Luke 4:29).

The message for us is twofold. Anyone who wants to fight injustice will meet opposition. Those who would struggle against oppression by nonviolent means will encounter a violent response.

The servant in Isaiah argues that we must strive to bring about a just world. But this will be achieved by personal moral renewal first. In the case of the servant it will also demand a sacrificial death (see Isaiah 52:13-53:12). Sin causes injustice. An atoning death removes the sin and leads to justice:

> If he gives his life as an offering for sin,
>   he shall see his descendants in a long life....
> Through his suffering, my servant shall justify
>   many.... (Isaiah 53:10b, 11b)

Jesus would exemplify this teaching by his own atoning death. He became a leader by serving the cause of justice and salvation. He is my Servant Leader.

In our century we have seen the spiritual power of nonviolent spirituality in the lives of Mahatma Gandhi, Rev. Dr. Martin Luther King, Jr., Archbishop Oscar Romero, the slain Jesuit priests and the women Church workers who died in Central America in the cause of justice. Anyone who espouses the cause of justice walks on dangerous ground, even more so when they work as apostles of peace.

Christ's plan for social ministry is found throughout the Gospels. His story of the Good Samaritan (Luke 10:29-37) calls us to tolerance for the outsiders and care for the stranger. His parable about the rich man and Lazarus (Luke 16:19-31) highlights the curse of indifference to social needs. Pope John Paul II frequently applies this parable to the social disorder in a world where rich nations ignore the plight of the poor ones, even plunder them to maintain their own high standards of living.

The most concrete teaching of Jesus on social ministry can be found in his depiction of the Last Judgment (Matthew 25:31-46). He proclaims that we will be judged by our response to the hungry, the thirsty, the stranger, the naked and the prisoner. "Amen, I say to you, whatever you did for one of these least brothers of mine, you did for me" (Matthew 25:40b). Here is a plan for social ministry that has guided Christians since then. Tradition embraces this passage as the seven "corporal works of mercy" and adds a companion seven, the "spiritual works of mercy." They all speak of our obligation to the individual in need; they also remind us of our call to bring justice to the world and of God's demand that we practice mercy beyond the obligations of justice.

The Corporal Works of Mercy

Feed the Hungry

Every night, even in this modern century, millions of people go to bed hungry. Countless numbers of these are children who suffer from starvation and malnutrition. TV gives us vivid images of children with swollen bellies and lines of people patiently waiting to get some food. The homeless wander the streets of the world's richest cities as well as the poor ones.

Jesus commands us to feed the hungry. In doing so we feed Christ himself. Failure to respond results in a negative judgment upon us: "Depart from me, you accursed, into the eternal fire prepared for the devil and his angels" (Matthew 25:41). This means more than providing food and handouts for the hungry in local soup kitchens or financing food shipments to the famished world. That is necessary indeed. But we must also lobby for laws and policies that will help local municipalities and poor nations to solve their food problems. Government has the duty to care for the common good. It should see that every sector of society, including the business world, contributes to that good. It is our obligation as Christians and citizens to see that the government does so.

Give Drink to the Thirsty

Jesus says that even giving a drink of water to a thirsty person in his name is a Christian obligation. In his desert culture that advice might seem more relevant than to our own society. But with the emergence of environmental concerns about the water supply, his counsel becomes very pertinent indeed. When our factories pollute the air and fill the rain with acid, when they pour their waste into the rivers and lakes and make the water undrinkable, they present a threat to our water supply.

When hospitals dump their surgical waste into the ocean, which washes it back to corrupt our beaches, they threaten our children with disease and prevent our rightful access to the shores. They must be made to realize their social responsibility to the common good. When states play politics with the water supply and menace other states with undue fears for their well-being, they act against the deceptively simple command of Jesus to give drink to the thirsty. In his encyclical letter *Centesimus Annus,* Pope John Paul II notes that when people discover their capacity to transform the world through their own work, they often forget this is always based on God's original gift of the things that are. The gifts of creation are meant for everyone's benefit and not for the selfish use of the powerful.

Clothe the Naked

When you live beyond your means to maintain a certain standard of living, you must borrow and go into debt. America has a mounting debt because it does not produce enough to sustain its standard of living. Its policies fail to motivate people to live thriftily and to accept a standard of living in line with what can be produced and paid for. Japan, envied as an economic titan, preserves its financial surplus by fostering high production and keeping people at a lower standard of living than they could afford. People who live beyond their means go into debt. Those who live austerely within their means have a surplus.

The difficulty in our country is not just an increasing debt, but also less money for education, medicine, family enhancement, job development and other services for the "naked"—that is, the poor, who are increasing in numbers in this wealthy nation. The drug and alcohol dependency and the rampant crime of all our major cities (and some smaller ones) are traceable to the despair of the underclass.

This despair arises from a sense of entrapment, especially in the major cities. Manufacturing jobs have departed for elsewhere; suburban companies will not hire the inner-city poor (who do not have transportation to get out there in any case). Housing policies favor wealthy gentrifiers; goods and services go to the rich and fail to reach the poor.

Can a nation live with an easy conscience when it is willing to go into deeper debt to pay for an unwarranted life-style, while the poor expand and become more "naked" than ever? Jesus says we should clothe the naked, that is, bring a just and decent life to the poor.

Shelter the Homeless

From New York to Rio the number of homeless people on the streets is increasing. It used to be that we thought this only happened in Calcutta. Yes, we have shelters for the homeless, but why not homes for them?

Misguided social policy drove truly mentally ill people to the streets with the promise that they could function on their own with "halfway" houses to aid their transition. To a great extent such temporary houses never materialized and many of the sick people were not able to care for themselves.

With growing poverty and broken families, single parents and their children are thrown onto the streets. The prosperous often play "blame the victim" for this mess. Politicians preach about "welfare queens" to keep the rest of us from looking deeper into the social system that is making homelessness a growing and inexcusable reality.

Every human being deserves the dignity and decency which comes from having a place to come home to, a place to call one's own. Jesus, who had no place to lay his own head, taught us to be concerned with the homeless. He was born in a stable, but he wants us to have a home and to shelter the homeless. This goes beyond financing city shelters. That is a stopgap measure.

There should be a systemic solution that eliminates the causes of homelessness. I do not pretend to have the practical answers to this challenge. I do think we have the knowledge and the money to do it. What we need is the moral strength and vision to make it possible. A Christian vision nourishes the will to change that we need. Jesus has given us the vision. Our job is to make it practical.

Visit the Sick

When an American state proposes a law to kill the terminally ill, Christ's command to visit and comfort them with hope is the proper Christian response. In our fragmented society, concern for the sick and the dying needs more attention. All sick people need and deserve loving care and whatever medical help is available. At the level of social policy some new method must be found to provide all citizens with reasonable health care.

At a personal level, the sick, especially the terminally ill, need our presence. Their suffering is not limited to physical pain. They also undergo the rude ordeal of a failing body, the decline of mental faculties and the humbling experience of depending on others. They are in the painful process of letting go of themselves, ripping themselves away from what meant so much to them, especially separation from family and loved ones.

As much as the physical pain, this will distress them and even drive them to despair if they experience no support in their crisis. Faith in a God who loves them and hope in the Resurrection will not exempt them from this suffering. Scripture tells us of many people in similar situations, particularly in the psalms of pain.

Our presence to the sick allows them to talk about their fears and desires, to break out of their loneliness and get some relief from their anxieties. It helps them to look back on their lives and see how things have turned out. Sick people, certainly those near the end, have great longings; communication with them can help. Our presence with them helps them reconcile with their past, their relatives and friends, themselves and God. It gives them a fresh outlook for the days that remain.

In becoming a companion with the sick on their journey through suffering, we witness the gospel and express our solidarity with them. Often the presence of Jesus is experienced by both the sick person and the one who is present. Communion with the sick and the dying is a privileged moment.

Ransom the Captive

The hostage crises we have experienced revitalize this call of Jesus. Hostages and political prisoners need more attention today as their numbers expand. Amnesty International has developed a variety of ways to keep the plight of political prisoners before our attention. Church groups and missionary societies serve much the same purpose. The liberation process is long, tedious, frustrating and often dangerous, as we saw in the cases of hostages held in Iran and Beirut.

Connected to this is the fight for human rights in countries where whole populations have been held captive by their own governments. Such human rights include: the right of political and religious freedom, the right to seek the truth, the right to an environment favorable to raising a family, the right to economic conditions that foster human dignity. In the free societies, we need to fight for the right of the unborn to life in this world. We are also called to struggle against racism, sexism and ageism. Ultimately, the source of these rights is religious freedom that permits us to live the truth of our faith in harmony with our dignity as persons.

Another dimension of this call is a concern for those in our prisons. Many Christians visit prisoners to show someone cares for them, to share their faith with them, to help them out of unjust situations, to pray with them, to plead for just treatment, to give them hope about the future. Active love never ceases in the Church. These ministries to prisoners, hostages and populations terrorized by their governments reflect the dynamism of our faith and are outstanding responses to Christ's call.

Bury the Dead

The burial of the dead is a social ministry and a communal event. The ceremonies of reverence and respect for the dead teach a great deal to the living and provide comfort to the bereaved. Someone should see that there is no financial exploitation of the closest survivors, vulnerable in their sorrow. Families should avoid vain extravagance that speaks more about their public image than of the importance of the deceased.

Christian hearts should reach out to the mourners—not just at the wake and the funeral, but all through the grieving process, which lingers for some time after the burial. Support groups for survivors are one way to fill this need. The process of grieving takes time. The more we are sensitive to the pain of loss others experience, the more we can help them through it to acceptance and relative peace. For some, the ache of loss never completely disappears. Religious mementos, prayers, Masses and Scripture-sharing have a powerful healing effect when wedded to personal kindness to the bereaved.

These seven paths to social ministry are practical expressions of being disciples of Jesus. They call us to heal the symptoms of poverty, injustice and suffering in the world. They also challenge us to heal the causes of systemic poverty and institutionalized injustice. Our Church has been outspoken on such matters in its social teachings. Every Pope from Leo XIII to John Paul II has addressed the social implications of the gospel. Jesus did not give us these ideas as bits of casual advice, as though they were not essential to being a Christian. He attached them to identification with himself. What we do to and for others, we do to him. He tied them to the judgment we will receive at the end of our lives. How we behave on these matters today has eternal consequences for us.

The Spiritual Works of Mercy

The demands of social ministry are not completed by the corporal works of mercy. The social gospel also includes the spiritual works of mercy. The whole person includes both body and soul. We have a social responsibility to the souls of others, just as to their bodies. The full social gospel demands this broader vision of ministry to the total personhood of others.

Jesus healed the sick, saved a woman faced with capital punishment, fed the multitudes, mourned at gravesides, defended the poor and stood up for the rights of the persecuted. He also brought meaning to people's lives, gave them a sense of confidence, drew people from their sinfulness, witnessed patience in suffering, forgave generously, consoled the sorrowing and taught us how to pray. He commanded us to be responsible for the spiritual needs of others.

Instruct the Ignorant

The title most often given to Jesus in the Gospels is "teacher." Jesus spoke of himself as the light and the truth. He was not interested in teaching people just facts, but also meaning. He talked about everyday matters, but showed their spiritual implications. The greatest ignorance is forgetfulness of our spiritual lives and our eternal destiny. Jesus addressed the moral aspect of decisions and the impact they have on the development of character and inner spirituality.

This is why the Church has a long history of involvement in education. The farmer-monks of the Benedictine Order taught agriculture to the barbarian tribes in the Dark Ages. The mendicant scholars of the Dominican and Franciscan Orders founded universities such as Oxford, Cambridge, Krakow, Paris and Padua in the high Middle Ages. Jesuits used drama as well as a classics curriculum to bring a genuinely Catholic education to believers of the Counter-Reformation. Missionary congregations

flooded the world of the nineteenth and early
twentieth century with parochial schools.

The Church has emphasized that there can be no
genuine education without God. Catholic schools also
teach the basics of learning for making one's way in
this world. There should be no contradiction between
the two. In the Third World today, Church-sponsored
education is seen as one of the best ways to lift people
from their poverty. The ministry to the mind is always
connected to the ministry to the heart, the salvation of
those we teach. This is an essential feature of the
social gospel.

Counsel the Doubtful

Jesus persistently summoned his hearers to faith.
For a variety of reasons the message from our culture
today is doubt, skepticism and the consequent loss of
confidence in self. The late Kenneth Clark, art
historian and host of the PBS television series
Civilization, when asked why great civilizations
declined, said that it was due to a loss of confidence
based on self-doubt.

Our social responsibility to a culture of doubt is
the witness of our faith in Jesus Christ. This is more
than scoring points against relativists. It means taking
seriously our personal call to a deep spirituality where
faith is nourished and made tough. It includes our
willingness to share our faith with others in word and
deed. A living faith is the best medicine for doubt. We
live in a beautiful civilization, despite its sins. If we
want to save it from its own loss of confidence, we
must bring it the dynamic gift of our faith. Thomas the

Apostle should be our mentor with his words to Jesus: "My Lord and my God!" (John 20:28b).

Admonish the Sinner

After Jesus saved the woman taken in adultery, he told her not to sin any more (see John 8:11b). He admonished her. In our time we have been bullied into being so nonjudgmental about sin that we act as though there is no personal sin. This is intellectual self-deception as well as moral cowardice. Of course, we should not rashly judge the sinfulness of others. That does not mean we leave our brains at the door and pretend there is no sin at all. Denying the existence of sin is a cultural fantasy that is just as self-destructive as other forms of denial.

We have a social responsibility to object not just to social sin but also to personal sin. Evil's greatest triumph is to fool us into believing it does not exist. This is a fool's paradise. All admonishing of sinners, whether in the public forum or in a private situation, should be done with a forgiving attitude and never with self-righteousness. Just because this has been done badly does not justify not doing it at all. Jesus spoke and acted plainly about sin. He loved the sinner but hated the sin. Whatever we do in this regard should be a reflection of his approach.

Bear Wrongs Patiently

Was anyone ever more unjustly treated in history than Jesus? His words of truth were maliciously used against him. His acts of kindness were brutally twisted to condemn him. He bore all this with patience and dignity. His Way of the Cross was a symphony of patience.

We may well be the most defensive culture in history. Impatience with opposition and personal affronts is our quick response. We have decided that suffering is the worst thing that could happen to us, so we do everything to defend ourselves against it. We spend a lot of energy and money avoiding pain as though it were an injustice. Our preoccupation with our "right" not to suffer has brought us to talk about a "right to die."

I do not object to reasonable efforts to ease physical pain, especially for the terminally ill. Nor do I oppose means taken to protect our reputations. But it is an illusion to think that suffering is the worst of ills or that it can be completely avoided. The witness of Jesus is the answer to the inevitable pain of living. He turned it into a redemptive act. He showed us the potential it has for forming character and growing spiritually. Our Christian witness to bearing wrongs patiently is another step in our social responsibility to our culture.

Forgive Offenses

Peter once asked Jesus if forgiving seven times was enough. Jesus said that seventy times seven was better. In other words, we should always be ready to forgive. The culture says that an apology is needed before forgiveness can be offered, that repentance should precede forgiveness. A Christian mind-set tells us that forgiveness makes repentance possible.

The culture practices "after-giveness"; Jesus calls for "before-giveness."

Our society has many intractable problems. All kinds of special interest groups have a multitude of grudges based on a history of injuries. Quite correctly, legal, economic and political means are being sought to redress these wrongs. But law does not change the heart. Money does not stifle the anger. Politics is not a unitive force. The attitude of forgiveness is the healing power that should accompany all these other legitimate efforts to achieve justice. We must have a reconciled and reconciling society if there is to be true and lasting justice.

Comfort the Afflicted

Jesus mourned with Martha and Mary at Lazarus' grave. He felt compassion for the family of Jairus, whose daughter had died. He empathized with the widow of Naim, whose teen-age son lay dead. He assured the Good Thief of a destiny in paradise. Jesus walked with people in their pain; he comforted the afflicted.

Any realistic assessment of our life on earth will tell us that it is a scene of abiding suffering, tragedy, pain and death. Children die in Christmas fires. Old people live in fear and hunger. Spouses have gut-wrenching quarrels. Teen-agers commit suicide. AIDS is a plague. We may have more lonely people than any society in living memory. Child abuse, sexual harassment, prejudice, murders and car accidents are commonplace.

We all know people who are hurting. They need our care. They need our time. They need us to accompany them in their suffering. This does not mean that they need our advice or that they are looking for magic words that will wipe away the tears. What they desire is someone to love them, to listen to their loud wails and complaints. Each of us can be a wailing wall like the one in Jerusalem, a place where the suffering can come and pour out their sorrows. We can give them hope by our presence. We are able to nourish their faith by our prayers. We can comfort them with our love.

Pray for the Living and the Dead

Prayer is communion with God. It is also communion with the living and the dead by the power of God. There may be techniques for praying, but prayer itself is not a technique. It is not an infallible method for getting our way, even for undeniably good causes. Prayer is a gift of the Holy Spirit. It grows silently until it becomes a habit of the heart. At that point prayer enables us to become sensitive to God's will. The most genuine prayer is always one that is in tune with the will of God.

Prayer must be practiced just as we would for acquiring other good habits. The easiest practice is the daily prayer for the living and the dead. Every day, consciously and deliberately, we should lift up to God the needs and concerns of our friends, relatives, acquaintances and the sufferings of other people in the world. This causes us to hold them all with God in our loving memory. It moves us to do what we can to help them achieve their goals.

The saints tell us that nothing is more powerful than prayer. They devoted hours each day to prayer and learned how to make all their deeds visible acts of prayer. St. Benedict told his monks that "to work is to pray." Prayer is another powerful means of taking seriously our social responsibility to others.

Conclusion

The social gospel is an essential part of Christianity. The struggle for justice and mercy is a constitutive (essential) aspect of gospel living. Our Servant Leader Jesus preached and witnessed responsibility to the world. Our review of the corporal and spiritual works of mercy clearly demonstrates the mosaic of possibilities for living the social gospel.

We are called to minister to the total human being, soul and body. We should be socially responsible for the political, economic and cultural order. We should equally be responsible for the spiritual needs of individuals and the culture. Our calling is all-encompassing:

All things are of your making.
All times and seasons obey your laws,
but you chose to create [us] in your own image,
setting [us] over the whole world in all its wonder.
(Preface for Sundays in Ordinary Time V)

Reflection

Advocates of the social gospel sometimes pay so much attention to ministering to the physical needs of others that they forget their responsibility to others' spiritual needs. The following exercises are designed to awaken a holistic vision of Christian social responsibility.

Feed the Hungry

What charities have I supported this past year?

How personally have I been involved in helping the poor?

What social causes do I advocate? In what way?

Give Drink to the Thirsty

What am I doing about environmental safety?

What do I do to protect our water supply?

Clothe the Naked

How far would I lower my standard of living to increase that of the poor?

What causes despair among the poor?

Shelter the Homeless

How have I helped homeless people recently?

What social policies do I think would eliminate homelessness? How can I help make these possible?

Visit the Sick

How do I find myself caring for sick people?

Is there a place for me in the hospice movement?

What do dying people need from me?

Ransom the Captive

Which human rights am I willing to stand up for?

How do I counter racism, sexism and ageism?

When have I ministered to prisoners?

Bury the Dead

What is my approach to grieving with the bereaved?

What has comforted me in the face of loss?

Instruct the Ignorant

In what way am I a Christian educator?

What benefits to the social order do I see coming

from an education that has religious and moral values?

Counsel the Doubtful

How confident am I that I can know the truth?

What means do I use to help others overcome their doubt and skepticism?

Admonish the Sinner

Why should I object to social and personal sin?

How can I avoid self-righteousness in a particular case?

Bear Wrongs Patiently

In the face of being wronged, am I a doormat or an armored personnel carrier? How should I react?

Who among the people I admire suffers wrongs patiently?

Forgive Offenses

How do I carry out Christ's command to forgive always?

Is there someone in my life I cannot bring myself to forgive? If so, what would make me change?

Comfort the Afflicted

How do I show compassion to those who are hurting?

What does it mean to say that I can be a personal "wailing wall" for others?

Pray for the Living and the Dead

Why shouldn't I think of prayer as a technique for getting my own way?

For whom do I pray? How often?

Prayer

Jesus, my Servant Leader, you call me to follow you by being responsible for the bodily and spiritual needs of others. Help me to think beyond the circle of my own awareness and personal needs. Awaken in me a heartfelt compassion for troubled people. Move me beyond preoccupation with myself to reach out to others with a helping hand and a warm heart. Lead me to bring your healing love to a broken world.

Chapter Seven

JESUS, MY SAVIOR

Conqueror of Evil

Danger ahead! I must alert, possibly alarm, my reader at this point. The next few pages will be unpleasant. I will be talking about Auschwitz and evil as the prelude to my reflection on Jesus as our Savior. My point is that the Good News of Jesus only makes sense if we face the bad news. We need to admit and acknowledge what Jesus liberates us from. If you wish to avoid the story of the painful bad news, pass over the first pages of this chapter and begin reading at the section about the Good News.

A Visit to Auschwitz

I came to Auschwitz on a warm and cloudless day. Groomed gardens and green trees surround the entrance. Grass and bushes border the brick buildings and streets of the camp. It had been a Polish army barracks before it was taken over by the Nazis. The barracks now serve as museums that chronicle the atrocities. The place looks deceptively attractive. The encounter with its reality is devastating.

Slowly, building by building, the story unfolds: pictures of train arrivals, frightened people, an officer facing newly arrived victims and deciding immediate death or temporary reprieve with a wave of his arm (right flick, the gas chambers—left flick, slave labor). Drawings show brawny prison guards dragging people by their hair, kicking them, beating them at will. The pictorial survey revives the terrible story.

The next set of revelations introduces the personal side of the tragedy. Reconstructions of typical dorms with mats, bunk beds, bathrooms and sinks disclose the dehumanizing conditions. I saw a bowl of soup with one crust of bread in it, a prisoner's only meal after a day of forced labor.

Then come the bins of human leftovers. Envision a hallway with large picture windows behind which you will see, in order, acres of human hair, a mountain of eyeglasses, an expanse of shoes (many of them children's shoes), a mound of suitcases marked with names, addresses and birthdays, a pyramid of opened Zyklon-B cans and a sample of the crystals in a bowl. This seems less like a tour than like a descent into hell.

I passed by a bandstand where musicians played to welcome the victims from the trains. The impression of normalcy was designed to trivialize the nightmare. There is ample evidence of the overwhelming percentage of Jews who were killed at this camp. There is also a record of the great number of Polish and gypsy Christians who died there.

I came to the death block, a U-shaped space where firing squads passed their days shooting people. I saw a picture of a man turning his face to the guns just as they were fired. To the right was death row, a basement prison where people were detained until execution. Down there I saw three chimney-like cells with an iron door at the bottom. Each night four prisoners were forced to crawl in there and stand upright in the dark space until morning. Then they returned to slave labor, pulling a cement roller to smooth out a new road.

Next to this I came to the cell of St. Maximilian Kolbe. He voluntarily took the place of a married man destined for starvation. Flowers and candles carpet his cell. Here is a sign of nobility, beauty and heaven in this human-made hell. Kolbe's humanity enhances the innocence of the millions of victims brutalized here.

Finally, the crematorium: It is a brick bunker sunk into the earth and covered with lawn. Huge chimneys rise out of it. The guards were fond of saying, "No one escapes here except through the chimney." The gas chamber is the first room, about the size of a classroom. The feel of death still broods in the air. The bodies were dragged from this vacuum-sealed room into one next door. There the space is relatively small. A covered iron tray on a waist-high counter received the bodies, which were then shoveled into the ovens. Behind the ovens are doors for removing the ashes. One still contains congealed human ashes.

Outside in the sunlight, I saw a wire fence about fifty feet from the entrance. Behind that fence once stood the house of the camp director, Rudolph Hess. His children played in the yard. Maids probably grumbled about the dust from the ashes. He hosted dinner parties there; his guests drank wine and ate lamb while the endless procession of the dead continued daily. At Nuremburg, he testified that he personally ordered the death of two million people.

Sin Is Bad for Our Health

I have never had a greater experience of the palpability of evil than at Auschwitz. It would be a mistake to say that it was caused by lunatics. It is better to state that it was caused by sin. Perhaps sin does craze the mind, but it is sin nonetheless. Sin harms persons. Never in history have so many millions been fatally harmed by so much malicious sinfulness. Our Jewish brothers and sisters are right in insisting that Auschwitz and other death camps be preserved. Let anyone who still does not believe in sin and immorality and evil go there and see firsthand.

I want to spend a little while exploring sin with you, for that is the condition for understanding the need for salvation. Sin is a complex issue. The angle I take here, that it is bad for our bodily, emotional and spiritual health, is only the tip of the iceberg. I concede there is much more to be said.

Before proceeding, I must make a distinction. My survey is about the reality of objective sin and its harmful results. I am not talking about the subjective sinfulness of any particular human being. Most writing in the last twenty-five years has been about that. I am fully aware that, subjectively, moral responsibility and malice varies with each person according to nature, nurture, psychological and social circumstances. Without a doubt, people sin—myself included. But my attention here is on the objective reality of sin, its effects and the need to be aware of it. I am not casting stones. I am looking at why stones are cast in the first place.

Sin Is Bad for Bodily and Emotional Health

Sin can kill people. Sin ultimately is a death act, as so terribly illustrated by Auschwitz. Sin is an evil force that results in self-destruction if it is not checked. Sin kills the unborn and moves some today to call for the killing of the elderly. When we are open to killing humans in the first six months of their existence (abortion) and in the last six months of life (euthanasia), we will soon be willing to kill them anytime. Sin causes death: "For the wages of sin is death" (Romans 6:23a).

Sin brings disease. Sexual promiscuity has generated a host of sexually transmitted diseases. For the first time in its history, the Center for Disease Control in Atlanta conducted a survey of the sexual habits of teenagers in 1991. Its most alarming finding discovered that forty percent of ninth graders are sexually active. By twelfth grade the number is seventy-two percent. The Center is worried about health epidemics. Yes, and we should also worry about the moral future of these young people.

Sin in the form of greed causes poverty in our society. When a major portion of our money floats to the top few in our culture, there is little left for those in the middle and on the bottom. Greed increases poverty, which in turn results in hunger and malnutrition, causing brain deficiencies in the children of the poor.

Sin as uncontrolled anger causes abuse of children and spouses. True, the cycle of abuse has a psychological dimension and therapy is needed, but at the root of it all is a sinfulness that has produced the neurosis. Karl Menninger has eloquently reminded us of this in his book, *Whatever Became of Sin?*

Sin is failure to love. This failure begets loneliness, alienation and personal emptiness. Sin sometimes appears as tyrannical pride that makes others feel worthless, inferior and resentful. Sin comes at other times as sloth, which engenders an emotional life that is dead and deprived of ambition and hope. The sin that tells us envy, jealousy, lust, unbridled anger and pride are OK is prescribing an emotional life destined for breakdown.

Sin Is Bad for Spiritual Health

Sin is an absence. It has no life of its own. It is a parasite that feeds on the goodness with which we were born. It is always a negative. That is why we speak of sin as an absence of the love of self, others and God. It is a state of "unlove." Therefore, sin destroys any possible spirituality that assumes love as the basic act. The ascendancy of sin wrecks relationships with self, others and God.

Sin blinds us to our divinely created origin, our destiny, our purpose for being alive at all. There can be no spirituality if we pay no attention to where we came from, where we are going and our divinely given purpose in life. Sin ruins our spiritual health.

We often hear today of the disappearance of faith in significant parts of Western culture. Sin is "unfaith" as well as unlove. The absence of religious faith in God, the loss of belief is the result of sin. Recall that I speak here only of objective sin, not its subjective side, not a given person's responsibility for unbelief. Read John 8:39-59, where Jesus shows how unbelief can be sin. Psychologist M. Scott Peck precisely captures the meaning embedded in that passage: "There are only two states of being: submission to God and goodness, or the refusal to submit to anything beyond one's own will—which refusal automatically enslaves one to the force of evil. We must ultimately belong either to God or the devil."

I will end here my sad chronicle of sin's effects. My point is that the self-destructiveness we see around us is ultimately caused by sin. Oftentimes, evil people destroy others rather than make the effort to get rid of the sin in their hearts. Many refuse to admit there is any sinfulness in their souls. They lie to themselves about it.

It is not accidental that examination of conscience is not a priority for those caught in sin. Scripture calls the devil the father of lies (see John 8:44). The pervasive self-deception about personal sinfulness proves the aptness of the scriptural observation. Too many people cherish the myth of their inner perfection and fail to see what is destroying them and others through them.

Enough, then, of this bad news. I highlighted it because the Good News of Jesus is God's response to the sin of the world. I believe we must look unflinchingly at our own consciences, throw away the fantasies of perfection, which are nothing more than comforting illusions, and open our hearts to Jesus Christ, who loves us enough to save us.

The Good News of Jesus

"[B]ehold, I proclaim to you good news of great joy that will be for all the people. For today in the city of David a savior has been born for you who is Messiah and Lord" (Luke 2:10b-11).

Before you go further in this chapter, stop reading and put on a recording of some Christmas carols. Close your eyes and listen to a choir such as Kings College of Cambridge. Hear their soul-melting rendition of "O Come, All Ye Faithful," "Silent Night," their unsurpassed presentation of "Once in Royal David's City."

Imagine a simple crib scene. Look at Mary and Joseph hovering over the child. Gaze at the shepherds intently focused on Jesus. Hear the songs of the angels. Watch the Magi present their gifts. Personalize the prayer of the mighty Christmas hymn and let its words enfold you. "O come, let me adore him, Christ my Lord." Use that for some centering prayer.

Why the Incarnation?

Time now to resume your reading.

The carols are people theology. The rich

melodies and inspired poetry tell us convincingly why the Son of God became a human being. If sin had been allowed to control the world, we would all be destined for eternal death. Sin would kill us here and hereafter. God loved us enough to stop that process and give us hope. "For God so loved the world that he gave his only Son, so that everyone who believes in him might not perish but might have eternal life" (John 3:16). Jesus was born in time to save us for eternity.

The Word was willing to become flesh to liberate us from sin's dominance and to honor the positive aspects of the body and the material world. Jesus showed us how our bodies and creation itself can be a theater where we sing God's praises and are rescued from any dishonesty about ourselves.

Scripture is very forthright about using the term flesh/body to describe the Incarnation. Philosophical and religious movements such as Gnosticism tried to pry Jesus away from his body and claim he was only a spirit wearing a costume of flesh. The author of John's Gospel fought that error by insisting that the Word became flesh (see John 1:14). The Son of God wanted it all, a body and a history in which to live.

> When peaceful silence lay over all,
> and night had run the half of her swift course,
> down from the heavens, from the royal throne
> leapt your all-powerful Word.... (Wisdom 18:14-15a,
> *Jerusalem Bible*)

Genesis tells us the story of the fall of humanity; Christmas sings of God descending. Humans fell miserably; the Word came down mercifully. We each fall through pride; the Word descended with humility and grace. The Word through whom all creation occurred is now himself created that he may walk among the lost and that the lost may be found.

The Fourth Eucharistic Prayer speaks of the event as the fullness of time. The Greeks spoke of two kinds of time: One is *chronos*, which means clock time, the chronological order. The other kind of time is *kairos*, which is spiritual time, quality time, fullness time, the "right time" for a new beginning. Christ's arrival in time was so much a kairos that history started over again. His birth occasioned a "born-again" history, hence we date our lives ever since from the birth of Jesus—the Year of our Lord, Anno Domini.

The first Adam had cast a shadow over history. The new Adam throws a rainbow of light over a new beginning of history. We had been dead in our sins. (Recall that sin kills.) Now we have new life in Jesus and have become a new creation. The Incarnation calls us to throw off our self-deception, remove any lying about our true selves and accept a new birth in Jesus. As St. Leo the Great urges us:

> Christian, remember your dignity, and now that you share in God's own nature, do not return by sin to your former base condition. Bear in mind who is your head and of whose body you are a member. Do not forget that you have been rescued from the power of darkness and brought into the light of God's kingdom.

> Through the sacrament of baptism you have become a temple of the Holy Spirit. Do not drive away so great a guest by evil conduct and become again a slave to the devil, for your liberty was bought by the blood of Christ.

Sin persuades us to lie to ourselves, to buy the illusion that there is nothing wrong with our souls. It consigns us to a dream state where we are asleep to our true reality. This lie is self-destructive and causes us to be a negative influence in our families and communities.

Jesus offers us the truth, the Good News about ourselves. He gives us the courage to admit we are imperfect. He holds us with love as he fills us with the daring to look at our sinfulness. Jesus is the truth that counters all the lies people live. As long as we lie to ourselves, there will be war within our hearts and trouble with those who meet us. Jesus invites us to be honest about our hearts. At Bethlehem Jesus emerged as truth in a human body.

The Revelation of Our Lovableness

Jesus also enables us to see what is really beautiful about ourselves, not just our sinful potential. We carry a great dignity: That is the true reason why Jesus came to us and why we are genuinely important. When we receive Jesus, who becomes the truth of our souls, he uncovers the image of God which our illusions hid from us.

The mystery grows deeper. Jesus asks us to see ourselves as images of the Son of God, as united to himself so that the Father sees him and us at the same time. When the priest pours some water into the wine at Mass, he praises God that we have been made sharers "in the divinity of Christ who humbled himself to share in our humanity" (Prayer at the

Preparation of the Altar and the Gifts).

The love the Father has for the Son is poured out on us as well. We are loved. God's Son came to us so we could recognize God's kindness. Our humanity is now his as well. Because of this, the goodness of God can never be hidden again. We began to see how lovable we really are when Love personified took on our humanity.

In reverencing the birth of our Savior, we celebrate our own new birth in him. "In him dwells the whole fullness of the deity bodily, and you share in this fullness in him" (Colossians 2:9-10a). In Jesus, the truth about being human has arisen in our bodies and justice has smiled on us from heaven. The fullness of time brought us the fullness of divinity.

The Gift of Peace

The scriptural texts about the Messiah ring with words of peace. The angels sing of peace to the shepherds. Isaiah's hymn to the Prince of Peace is heard again. So long as sin ruled our hearts we could have no inner peace. Before the birth of Jesus the angels wept because people thirsted for peace of heart but could not achieve it. In the shepherds' field the angels laughed with joy because peace of heart (the condition for world peace) is now possible for us. St. Bernard expands with his usual eloquence on this truth:

> Notice that peace is not promised but sent to us; it is no longer deferred; it is given; peace is not prophesied but achieved. It is as if God the Father

sent upon the earth a purse full of his mercy. This purse was burst open during the Lord's passion to pour forth its hidden contents—the price of our redemption. It was only a small purse, but it was very full. As the Scriptures tell us, *A little child has been given to us, but in him dwells all the fullness of the divine nature.*

Scriptural peace (the term is *shalom*) is a word that tells us of reconciliation between ourselves and God. That peace reconciles us to ourselves and each other. Sin divides us; Christ's peace unites us. Sin tears us apart; Jesus heals us and puts us together again. Sin makes us feel miserable about ourselves. Jesus makes us feel his goodness, which is now fused with the goodness he planted in us as the Word of God when he created us. We thus experience an oceanic peace that has silent depths. This is a creative peace that makes us reconciling persons for families, friends and the world. Now that we know how much God cares about us personally, we become aware of how much he thinks of all of us and feels for all of us. The unimaginable has happened. God has added humanity to his divinity and brought us the possibility of peace.

'The Glory of the Lord Shines Upon You' (Isaiah 60:1)

One image that permeates the readings and carols celebrating the Incarnation is the light of divine glory. The spiritual application of this teaching is well expressed by St. Paul:

...[T]he god of this age has blinded the minds of the unbelievers, so that they may not see the light of the gospel of the glory of Christ, who is the image of God.... For God...has shone in our hearts to bring to light the knowledge of the glory of God on the face of [Jesus] Christ.... But we have the mind of Christ. (2 Corinthians 4:4,6; 1 Corinthians 2:16b)

Salvation enables Jesus to live in our hearts and minds. His consciousness can exist within us; our awareness can commune with his. Jesus ceases to be an academic topic which we study. He becomes a person with whom we can commune because he is as close to us as we are to ourselves. We can possess the mind of Jesus in an experience of unity. The spiritual nature of this awareness allows for a permeability, a fusion of two awarenesses, two minds, in a union of such ease that "effortless" is the best way to describe it.

All of this occurs in an environment of freedom. Jesus has no need to control us. We do not approach him as passive dependents. To have the mind of Jesus is not a form of spiritual brainwashing. Instead, it is a dialogue of love which sustains the freedom of our communion. We freely surrender our minds and hearts to him, but only because we repossess ourselves as we truly are.

Scripture consistently describes such an experience in terms of glory and light, exactly as Paul did for the Corinthians. The scriptural word *glory* is a term for the experience of God's presence. The effect of glory is light—intuitional understanding of God's truth and love. This is not a sphere for words. This is the room of the Word who wordlessly shares with us the mind of God and the love which moves God to care for us and the world.

Paul told the Corinthians that those who are committed to the god of this transitory culture are blinded by him. They fail to see the glory of the real God and never know the light that would give them intuitional entry into his mind and love. The gospel remains veiled to them because they have not come to faith in Jesus.

For those who have faith in Jesus the light that comes from the experience of his glory-presence is a sure moral guide for the pursuit of goodness. Our minds begin to think about life as Jesus does. Our hearts fill with love for others just as the heart of Jesus does. Our wills, surrendered to the divine purpose, firmly embrace the good and reject sin and evil. This is the moral result of our spiritual union with Jesus. Our emotions are enlisted in the service of virtue instead of being wild horses that pull us chaotically into errant behavior.

We begin to see that Jesus is good for our bodily, emotional and spiritual health. Sin leads to greed, death and disease. Jesus leads us to simplicity, life and health. Sin generates self-destructive lust, angry abuse, sloth and all kinds of emotional pain. Jesus turns us toward a clean heart, a passion for justice, an energy placed at the service of mercy and emotional health. Sin kills love and spirituality. Jesus introduces us to a love that conquers all and a spiritual life in which we are led by the very Spirit of Jesus.

This is Christ's Good News, his answer to the self-inflicted harm that comes from sin. At the same time, the gospel does not deliver us completely from bodily, emotional and spiritual distress. We will still suffer from the harm resulting from the sin of others and from the impact of sin on the world and human nature. We will still get bodily illness (the common cold will never desert us), maybe a neurosis, certainly grief from the harassment of others. Death will come for us all, and we will sometimes know a spiritual aridity that makes us think God has abandoned us. We will continue to suffer in a variety of painful and unexpected ways.

This is the mystery of suffering. Jesus liberates us from the blindness and domination of sin, but not from all of its effects as long as we live in this vale of tears. The difference from our former life and now is that we have an inner zone of peace and love, hope and confidence that did not exist before. We have acquired a capacity to love and fight against the evils of the world which was heretofore non-existent. We will be positive contributors to the hope of the race and partners with other people in the search for love, justice and mercy.

With Paul we will beg God to deliver us from our suffering. "Therefore, that I might not become too elated, a thorn in the flesh was given to me, an angel of Satan, to beat me, to keep me from being too elated" (2 Corinthians 12:7b). Paul pleaded with God to be spared this suffering and heard God tell him no: "My grace is sufficient for you, for power is made perfect in weakness" (2 Corinthians 12:9b). In other words, we will have unnecessary, self-inflicted pain due to our sin, which is destructive and robs us of meaning and purpose in life. Then there is the unavoidable pain of living, which can be a source of spiritual power that makes our pride crumble and our lives be part of God's plan to redeem the world.

We could never know this unless Jesus had first shown us in his own suffering and death and the uses of pain for liberation from evil. Sin, which caused this mess in the first place, is destroyed by the very misery it engendered. This is why we need regular meditation on the cross of Jesus, for no problem bothers us more than the existence of suffering in the world. We shall never solve it with logic and philosophy. Only faith and identification with Jesus' cross gradually reveals to us why we will continue to suffer even after our conversion to grace.

This is the reason that John's Gospel connects the lifting up of Jesus on the cross to his lifting up to glory. In the Johannine vision the two liftings are one act. The death of Jesus on the cross is at once the revelation of his glory, a radically new and permanent experience of God's presence to the world. In Mark's Gospel this is expressed by the exclamation of the soldier as soon as Jesus dies: "Truly this man was the Son of God!" (Mark 15:39b).

The Carmelite Convent at Auschwitz

I want to share one other experience I had at Auschwitz. As soon as I drove from the entrance of the camp, I made a left turn and drove one block. There I came to a handsome, red brick building surrounded by a lovely garden about the size of a tennis court. A chain link fence encloses the complex and a speaker phone is at the gate. The back wall of the building is up against the outside wall of the death camp. There are no crosses on the building or any sign of its religious nature. It is the controversial Carmelite convent. Dialogue between Jewish leaders and Catholic bishops has resulted in a decision that the community will be transferred to a different location.

I was given admission to the convent chapel, where I saw an image that puts the bad news about Auschwitz and sin into the context of Good News and grace. Over the altar is a wall-to-wall fresco depicting the lines of the camp's victims headed for death. The coloring is chalklike—pale gray, soft pink, whitish gold. The figures are wraiths, more like ghosts or souls huddled on a forced march.

At the extreme right and left edges of the fresco, the people walk in darkness. At the center of the picture is the foot of the sanctuary cross. As the people get nearer to it, they encounter life, light and hope. The grays become gold. The somber dark tints acquire the pinkness of new life. The people journey to the Redeemer.

St. Paul writes, "...[W]here sin increased, grace overflowed all the more" (Romans 5:20b). This is the message of that touching fresco. Jesus, my Savior, is the response to sin even in its most terrible form. The sacred will overcome the demonic. God's love is more powerful than evil. "In him we have redemption by his blood, the forgiveness of transgressions, in accord with the riches of his grace that he lavished upon us" (Ephesians 1:7-8a).

Reflection

Jesus came as our Savior. The world has never been the same again. His Good News is meant to overcome our bad news. The following two exercises will help you examine yourself and then meditate on the graces and gifts of Christ's salvation.

What Is the Bad News in My Life?

How honest am I about my motives? Do I lie to myself?

What bodily habits do I have which are self-destructive? What steps do I or should I take to change?

On a scale of one to ten, in which one stands for weakness and ten for strength, where do I fit on matters of pride, lust, anger, sloth, gluttony, envy, greed? What will I do about the weak points?

Sin is the absence of love of self, others and God. It harms me and often moves me to harm others. If there is such an absence of love in my life, how do I know it? Why did this happen? How can I be saved?

Jesus can bring me peace of heart. What causes a lack of such peace in my life? How do I get in touch with the peace of Jesus?

Jesus is glory and light. How is he glory for me? How does his light affect my mind and heart? Has Jesus given me a new appreciation of a Scripture text? Has he filled my heart with deeper love for someone I found difficult to relate to?

Do I try to improve myself without reference to Jesus? If so, what strategies do I use? Why do I not turn to Jesus for inner peace and strength and a creative outlook on life?

An Exercise for Turning to Jesus in Faith

Read John 4:1-42, wherein a Samaritan woman spends some quality time with Jesus. He is a stranger to her. She fears him. She carries a lot of hurt in her heart because she has been betrayed in love so often. She has not faced her own responsibility for the loss of meaning and love in her life. She is empty. She has come to fill a water jar, but she has a void in her heart.

Jesus enters her life and invites her to change. He does this in several steps. See how these steps appear in his dialogue with her.

> He creates a mood of trust.
>
> He lets her know he is aware of her inner turmoil.
>
> He offers her new possibilities.
>
> He confronts her with her moral problems.
>
> He reveals himself as Messiah and invites her to faith.

What aspects of this dialogue ring true in your own experience?

Fill a glass with water and look at it meditatively.
Touch the water and note your reaction. Take a sip
and praise God for water. Then think of what Jesus
said about water and life and being filled. What is that
saying to you? Where will you go with your life today
because of this meditation?

Prayer

Jesus, my Savior, I bless you for coming to the world.
It can never be the same again because you have
come. Awaken me to whatever self-deception and
self-destructive behavior there may be in my life. Lead
me to be honest about myself. Live in my mind that I
may think as you think. Live in my heart that I may
love as you love. Take my feelings and use them in
your service. I praise you. I love you.

Chapter Eight

JESUS, MY EVANGELIZER

Spreading the Gospel

Find a man who has his mind made up and thousands will flock to his leadership. I discovered such a man in Paulist Father Alvin Illig. Single-handedly, he put evangelization on the agenda of the Catholic Church in the United States. It was my good fortune to work closely with him on a number of related projects.

Father Illig always saw the connection between evangelization and catechesis, and that was the connection that brought us together. He asked me to write a catechism for adults that could be used for convert instructions and also be incorporated into the Rite of Christian Initiation of Adults. Over the years we cooperated on a number of other projects.

Alvin was proud of the fact that he was in the first group of seminarians to be ordained by Bishop Fulton Sheen. He admired Sheen's preaching ability as well as his desire to share our Catholic faith with the world outside our Church. Alvin knew that a love of Scripture was the best way to generate an evangelizing spirit. This led him to enlist the hugely talented Father Larry Brett to create the "Share the Word" program which linked Scripture study and prayer to the Sunday liturgical readings.

Alvin was a practical man who knew how to take religion out of the scholar's tower and bring it to the parish church and the marketplace. Fascinated by the possibilities of the new media, he pioneered national evangelization meetings using satellite technology. He also sponsored the making of videocassette programs on Scripture. For him, the communications revolution was a gift from God to share the message of Christ. As he often said, "I take the electronic word to proclaim the divine Word."

Alvin lived by the dictum, "I don't want to be so heavenly minded that I'm no earthly good." His clear vision served his deep faith: "Will the goal and you will find the means to achieve it." He never believed in panaceas. To him there was no one right way to evangelize, just a marvelous variety of methods depending on the situation. Like his beloved St. Paul, patron of his congregation, he raced along with his culture to give the world the prize of Christ's salvation.

Breathless, the rest of us tried to keep up with him. He died on the eve of a national meeting of Catholic evangelizers in Washington, D.C. In my imagination I see Alvin trying to send us memos from his well deserved resting place with the Jesus he loved so well. His story makes an excellent introduction to our reflection on Jesus, my evangelizer.

The Great Commission

All four Gospels conclude with Christ's commission to evangelize the world. This "multiple attestation" demonstrates the essential importance of the mission to evangelize. These four commands to evangelize have two elements in common: (1) Go to everyone. (2) Don't do it alone, but go forth in the power of the Holy Spirit. The missionary drive of the Church is the source of its dynamism. When the Church loses this enthusiasm it lapses into a crisis of faith. Mission deeds renew the Church, revitalize the faith and sharpen Christian identity. My faith grows stronger when I share it with others.

Each Gospel sheds a different light on our evangelizing task.

Mark

Mark says, "Proclaim the gospel" (16:15b); share the person and message of Jesus to invite people to faith. But I cannot share the message of Jesus in the Gospels if I am not familiar with it. I will not communicate Jesus to others if I do not know him, and the best place to find him is in the Gospels. My familiarity with the Gospels is a condition for acquiring an evangelizing spirit. I should share the person and message of Jesus with others so that they can be invited to faith in him. Mark's aim was to lead his readers to the faith of Peter, who said, "You are the Messiah" (8:29c). Mark wants us to join the centurion at the cross in exclaiming, "Truly this man was the Son of God!" (15:39b), to share the gospel in order to invite others to faith in Jesus.

Matthew

Matthew tells us to bring people to the Church and the sacraments (see Matthew 28:19). Matthew's Gospel is the ecclesiastical one. It is the Gospel that speaks of the institutional Church, not in a cold organizational fashion, but as a structure for celebrating the mysteries of salvation and teaching its meaning.

Look at the scene Matthew evokes at Caesarea Phillipi (16:13-19). Jesus and the apostles gaze at the great Roman palace built on a rock. That calm solid building speaks of Roman continuity and order. Down below, near where they stand, is a cave sealed with a thick, iron gate. This is the shrine of the god Pan, the god of disorder and pandemonium. The heavy gate keeps back the mythological "chaos." Pacifying, sacrificial offerings border the outside of the shrine.

Jesus uses these two visual aids to speak to the apostles about an essential trait of his Church. It will be built on the rock of order. The gates of hell (disorder) will not prevail against it. He appoints Simon bar Jonah to be the leader of this Church and gives him a name to symbolize that: Peter—Rock (see 16:18). Why a Church? So that people will have a visible sign of salvation, a community to belong to, a setting where salvation continually happens.

Turn now to the scene at the conclusion of Matthew's Gospel (28:16-20). The risen Jesus meets with his apostles on a mountain. He commissions them to evangelize the world. They are to baptize the converts and teach them to observe all that Jesus has taught. In other words, sacraments and catechesis are connected to evangelizing. In Matthew's vision, evangelizing is a call to belong to the Church of Jesus, where salvation will be experienced in sacramental celebration and catechetical enlightenment.

Luke

Luke tells us to call people to conversion and to bear witness (see 24:44-48). Only the evangelized can evangelize. Only the convinced will convince others. The converted convert. Jesus wants his evangelizers to bear witness to his person and message to every human being. Witnesses practice what they preach. The credibility of the gospel depends on the believability of the communicator. This is more than theatrical pretense. This must be personal sincerity based on purity of life and a lifelong, developing relationship with Jesus. Cold evangelizers depend on technique. Hot ones draw their fire from the Holy Spirit, with whom they are in daily touch.

Such evangelizing is never proselytizing based on force or manipulation. It flows from the creative authority of Jesus. The word *force* comes from the Latin *potestas* and denotes compulsion based on superior strength, be that physical, moral or legal. *Authority*, on the other hand, comes from the Latin *auctor*, "author." It denotes a creative, inventive and inviting act. A witness does not force. A witness invites conversion by reason of the authority of the person's life and conviction.

An evangelizer can become a witness because of

the transforming power of the Holy Spirit. This is evident in the first fervor one often sees in a new convert. But there must be a second, a third, a thousandth conversion. It is a process that never ends. First fervor cools. It must be heated up again by continuing conversion through prayer, sacraments and acts of loving concern for others—such as described in our reflection on the corporal and spiritual works in Chapter Six. Conversion is a liberation from oppression in all its forms, especially from sin. The act of liberation is always spiritual, never a violent act against another. We follow the nonviolent cross of Jesus. Look again at our meditation, "Jesus, My Mentor" (Chapter Five), to see the process of conversion from the ego to the I to the not-I, in which Jesus becomes the driving center of our lives. That is the key to becoming an effective evangelizer in the Lucan sense.

John

John says to accept evangelizing as a mission. John introduces us to the experience of evangelizing as "being sent." We do not think up the idea on our own. We do not head out trusting in our own credentials. We go forth because someone has sent us. That someone is Jesus: "As the Father has sent me, so I send you" (20:21b). The process of sending begins with the Father, who sends Jesus to evangelize us. Then Jesus sends us, through the call of the Church, to evangelize others.

We can count on John's view to counter any excessive institutionalism that one might draw from

Matthew. John takes evangelizers into the mysterious life of God as the goal of their work. Evangelizers should lead people to eternal life and to the kind of love that exists between the Father and the Son. John's Jesus says, "Now this is eternal life, that they know you, the only true God, and the one whom you sent, Jesus Christ" (17:3). Here is a vision of Church that begins with love between divine Persons, a love that assures the inner unity of the Church. This love is the model and source of all the other unity people look for when they join the Church. Evangelizers will find this one of the most appealing motivations to potential converts.

Salvation and Kingdom

Jesus, Church, sacraments, catechesis, conversion, witness, mission—these are constant themes for evangelizers. But there are two master concepts associated with evangelizing: salvation and Kingdom. Salvation means that Jesus has come to free us from all that oppresses us, above all from sin. In our meditation, "Jesus, My Savior" (Chapter Seven), we explored that truth in terms of the Incarnation. The liturgies of Advent, Christmas and Epiphany help us to see our need for a Savior and how the Son of God responded to our deepest desire for spiritual liberation from sin. The liturgies of Lent, Holy Week, Easter and Pentecost take us through the process of salvation as accomplished by Jesus in his passion, death, resurrection and sending of the Spirit.

The result of salvation is the gift of Christ's

Kingdom. Matthew's Gospel gives us the most extensive understanding of what *Kingdom* means. It is a divine reality which has a partial earthly fulfillment and a permanent heavenly one. It brings love, justice and mercy to our earthly existence. It endows us with eternal life in our heavenly one.

It is a mistake to equate Christ's Kingdom with goals that are purely political, economic and cultural. That would put religion at the service of ideology. But when Christ's Kingdom transforms the human heart with love, justice and mercy, then the possibilities of a Christian society with political freedom, economic justice and cultural humanism are encouraged and advanced. Kingdom and society are related though not identified. Jesus told Pilate that his Kingdom was not of this world (see John 18:36). At the same time, his Kingdom serves the legitimate hopes of the world. Therefore evangelizers proclaim the Kingdom in terms of the Social Gospel as I described it in Chapter Six.

Obstacles to Evangelizing

Why is it so hard to evangelize? The difficulties which face evangelizers vary in different countries and cultures. I will confine my comments about obstacles to evangelizing in the United States. If the prospect daunts us, we need only recall what Jesus faced when he tried to evangelize. He gave up his life for the cause. So also did most of the apostles and all kinds of missionaries over the centuries. My list of six obstacles begins with the least problematic and ends with the most serious.

Cultural Obstacles

It has often been said that today's Americans get most of their knowledge of religion from the media. Frequently, that comes in the form of polls—bean-counting, in the argot of the trade. Just before the 1987 pastoral visit of Pope John Paul II to the United States, *Time* published a cover story about the event. On the cover the Pope is riding the "barque of Peter" in rough seas. Catholics on the American coast are shown in a restless mood as though at a street demonstration. The headline trumpets, "Pope Visits Feisty Flock."

The article was built around the results of a poll taken of Catholics on a variety of hot topics. The poll's results left the impression of discontented Catholics disagreeing with Church teaching on issues such as abortion, divorce and papal authority. The writers of the article seemed to instruct the readers—especially Catholic ones—that the pope and bishops should listen to the polls and adapt their teachings. After I finished it, I thought, "If Jesus had first taken a poll of the opinions on morality in Galilee, he probably would not have given the Sermon on the Mount."

Bean-counting is thin ice upon which to build a system of policy and teaching. I surely believe authority has a duty to listen to people's complaints, opinions and suggestions for change. Shared responsibility for the life of the Church is a good idea. Authority should sponsor constructive change where it is possible. But if a suggested change regards the teaching of Jesus, then it must be courteously, responsibly and resolutely rejected.

I call the poll-taking approach to faith an obstacle because it is too superficial when applied to the complex and deeply spiritual matters at stake.

Psychological Roadblocks

A few years ago, Air Force Chaplain Ed Deimeke asked me to present the subject of evangelization to a nationwide group of military chaplains and their assistants. I presented my material in a TV studio. The program was beamed by satellite to a number of locations around the country. The viewers were able to make comments and ask questions after the speech.

I was the second presenter in this new program. The first one was TV evangelist Robert Schuller. Chaplain Deimeke gave me a video of Schuller's presentation so I could see how he handled matters. Schuller began with the story of how he began his evangelizing mission. He is a member of the Dutch Reformed Church. In addition to his seminary training he had studied clinical psychology in his college years. He said that at his ordination to the ministry, he swore to uphold and share the teachings of the Heidelberg Catechism.

Then he was missioned to Garden Grove, California, to start a new parish there. He said he rang over three thousand doorbells before he felt ready to begin his ministry. He concluded that the most pressing need he discovered was a poor self-image among most of those he met. His psychological studies had alerted him to this problem, which affects many people.

Schuller decided that he would build his evangelizing mission around ministering to people's need to have a better sense of self-worth. The Jesus he would offer them was one who would help them feel better about themselves. Schuller packaged this message in his famous "possibility thinking" approach. Anyone who has watched his *Hour of Power* knows that is exactly what he has done for many years.

I think Schuller has a good point. While I would not focus my whole ministry on that theme, I do think it is a piece of the puzzle. Evangelizers should be aware of the self-worth problem, which can block a person's ability to come to Christ.

A good evangelizer will present a Jesus who honors and perfects the freedom and human dignity of each person. Jesus believes in the precious value of each person as an image of God and one worthy of divine love and salvation. An evangelizer who fails to minister to this need will have a difficult time converting the person. Worse yet, an evangelizer who makes a person with a rotten self-image feel even worse has no chance of getting through at all. Christ's Good News says people really are worthy of boundless love.

Sociological Pitfalls

A third obstacle to evangelizing is individualism. This characterizes the people who identify themselves in terms of function ("I am what I do") and possession ("I am what I own"). Status and wealth are very strong illusions. At the height of fame or in the full flood of money these people are in la-la-land. Experience has not yet taught them the fleeting fickleness of popularity—hero today and gone tomorrow. Time has not taught them the vanity of wealth. (The best biblical book on this topic is Ecclesiastes. No other book of the Bible better describes the foolishness of today's radical individualists.)

They are tough nuts to crack for an evangelizer who wants to call them to community, responsibility for others and to a list of values that includes the loss of self, bearing the cross and following Jesus. They think they have found heaven on earth, so why should they bother with one somewhere else? They *can* be reached and converted, but not without blood, sweat, tears, prayer and fasting. There will be more failures than successes. But one success alone makes the angels sing.

Anthropological Dead Ends

Another hardy resister to evangelization is the true believer in the sexual revolution. This acolyte has bought the package that says sex should be separated from children, and sex should not be attached to marriage. Today's sexual ideology is anti-child and anti-marriage. For those who are married, it teaches that intimacy and its pleasures should be preferred to the bother of children. So practice child prevention by contraception and abortion.

For those who are not married, it counsels affairs and temporary live-together arrangements. The result is the waning of family life and an alarming dip below zero population growth. Followed rigorously to its logical conclusion, the sexual revolution is a suicidal idea. Happily, a great many do not subscribe to it.

Evangelizers run into two problems here. First, the listeners will not like Jesus' teachings about sexuality, family and marriage. Secondly, the erosion of the family, which traditionally has been a center for the experience of the sacred, is rendering people so deaf to spiritual realities, so blind to religious values that an evangelizer encounters little that could be a starting point for dialogue. No obstacle, however, is insurmountable. Jesus retains extraordinary power to attract people and appeal to their hearts. The gospel contains a magnetism that will draw the most resistant. The Holy Spirit knows how to melt a glacier.

Philosophical Breakdowns

Western civilization was built on the Hebrew-Christian Bible and the philosophy of the Greeks. The Bible stressed the importance of conscience; the Greeks prized the value of reason. Scripture taught us who we should be; philosophy instructed us on the nature of being. Both teaching streams emphasized the objective nature of reality. For Jews and Christians, God was a person, a real, objective Other. We were expected to conform our lives to God. The Greeks viewed truth as an objective reality. If the mind expected to grow, it should conform itself to that truth.

The modern West has abandoned that ideal. The ancients said, "Conform your souls to reality." The moderns say, "Conform reality to your soul." What happened? Without explaining the history of how this occurred, I would simply state that our view of reality changed. Reality used to be thought of as something superior to the human: for example, God and absolute truth. Now, reality is nature, something inferior to the human. Formerly, we adored a God and reverenced nature. Today, we worship ourselves and manipulate nature. The faith, hope and love we focused on God has been changed into a rational use of technology to suit our needs and tastes.

Something else fell through the cracks: namely, the conviction about the objective order of things. What is left? The subjective view of life. This is why we have relativism. This is the origin of replacing truth with opinion. When only the subjective exists, then each person is the owner of some "personal" truth, actually just an opinion. Instead of the happy hum of philosophers discussing truth, there is only the cacophony of the marketplace of ideas.

In this situation evangelizers face a stubborn obstacle indeed. After all, evangelizers claim to share a message of truth and a person who literally claimed to be the truth. Yet even this is not a challenge impossible to overcome. Paul VI has said we must learn to trust explicitly the power of the gospel to convert people.

We may think we should become clever arguers to outsmart our relativist adversaries. I admit there is room for lively controversy here. But in the end we are asking for a religious response of faith. We must let heart speak to heart. We need to believe in the hidden energy of the gospel, which has its own power of persuasion. We are little more than spiritual brokers in a mysterious exchange between God and the other person. The more we learn to trust in the Spirit as the real evangelizer here, the more breakthroughs we will witness.

The Religious Ruin

Some people like to dialogue with nonbelievers without ever mentioning Jesus. This reminds me of the first ads that were aired about a new car, Infiniti. On the TV screen came a vast ocean, then waves surging to the shore, some soft, New Age music and a soothing voice talking about an experience that awaited the viewer. Nothing was said about Infiniti, not any car. I only knew this was a car ad because I read about it in a magazine article that questioned the wisdom of asking someone to buy a product that is never named. I haven't heard how the ad succeeded, but it seemed silly to me. I would say the same about the hypersensitive people who fear to mention Jesus to nonbelievers lest it offend their sensibilities.

This is all the more absurd in a culture which allows scatological language on family time TV. We have become tolerant of the most lurid language in public media, yet some of us grow faint at talking about Jesus to a prospective convert. This is reverse pornography. The tittilating has become sacred, but the sacred has become taboo. If Jesus becomes a "missing person" in the dialogue of salvation, then abandon all hope.

Of course, there is absolutely no need to avoid mentioning Jesus' name. Besides, it is counterproductive. If I never mention the one I love, the person I wish to convince may rightly suspect that my affection is shallow. My dear friend Alvin Illig insisted that we should always be willing to make the case for Christ even to devout nonbelievers. We don't have to be pompous, superior or belittling of others. Nor do we need to be contentious about it. We are not lawyers arguing a case or merchants closing a sale. We are ministers of the Holy Spirit serving the love of God in a dialogue of hearts.

The Holy Spirit Is the Lead Agent

The six cultural obstacles to effective evangelization may tempt us to scramble for the best techniques to overcome them. We have a childlike trust that techniques solve problems. Techniques do have some modest uses in this process. But evangelization is more concerned with the mystery of persons than with the problems which may stand between Christ and them. A person may have problems, but a person is a mystery, not a problem. If I look at a person as a problem, I will feel the urge to find solutions. If I consider a person to be a mystery, then I will approach him or her with reverence.

When I possess this reverential view of a person, I will be more prepared to allow the Holy Spirit to be the lead agent in the process. My principal guidelines will be faith and prayer. I will understand that faith is a better weapon than logic. I will appreciate that prayer is superior to persuasion. I should think of myself as a musical instrument open at both ends—a flute, perhaps. My voice and humanity will be seen and heard. But the breath of the Spirit will enter the flute and come forth as music to charm the person to conversion.

Read the Acts of the Apostles for numerous case studies of evangelization. The book provides summaries of six missionary talks to the Jews (2:14-36; 3:12-16; 4:8-12; 5:29-32; 10:34-43; 13:16-41). The themes are unambiguously supernatural. The apostles call people to faith in Jesus. The Spirit is given credit for the conversions and transformations. Read further about the expansion of the Church to the Gentile missions (13:44-52). The missionaries tell us it was the Spirit who impelled them to go beyond the Jewish population. They acknowledge that the Spirit gave them the boldness and courage to do what they otherwise would sensibly have avoided. The whole mission effort is Spirit-driven.

This is the perfect response to the mystery of the human person. The dialogue must be spiritual. The positive outcome will always involve the Holy Spirit. In retrospect there is no human accounting for the incredible advance of the apostolic Church. That is why we call the result a moral miracle and praise the Holy Spirit for making it happen.

Restoring the Romance

The theme of evangelization takes us back to the roots of our faith. Jesus was the original evangelizer.

His Good News of salvation and Kingdom, Church, sacraments and the gift of the Spirit converted the apostles and disciples. They became the next evangelizers, for the evangelized become the evangelizers. The converted make the most enthusiastic converters.

After twenty centuries of this process we have inherited a structure and a community of over one billion people. Our self-preservation instincts move us to conserve what we have. We are in the maintenance mode. The average diocese and parish spends close to ninety-nine percent of its money and human effort in keeping what we've got. But a maintenance mentality causes us to be stagnant and introduces a crisis of faith. Evangelization is the escape hatch from this complacent and self-destructive behavior.

Evangelization restores the excitement—yes, even the romance—of being a Catholic. Billions of people have not yet heard of Christ. Think of China alone. Millions that did know him in what were once Christian countries have forgotten him. In the United States alone there are close to ninety million unchurched people, children of God whose lives are not shaped by Jesus.

We have become a *pusillus grex*, a timid flock. We should be a joyful and courageous procession of the redeemed, carrying the cross and the banner of the Lamb that was slain and risen. Let the Spirit pipe a tune within us to charm the world to Jesus.

Reflection

Who is the first person that should be evangelized? You. Me. Evangelization of active Church members is the first step. Each of us needs the renewal in the Holy Spirit to swell the enthusiasm we need to share our faith in Jesus with others. Once my heart is full, my lips will sing. The following exercises deal with self-evangelization and the outreach to others.

Take Your Spiritual Temperature

In what ways is Jesus a "missing person" in my life?

When was the last time I felt I had a spiritual and moral conversion?

From what forms of sinfulness do I need to be saved?

How much has Christ's Kingdom of love, justice and mercy taken hold in my life?

Which of my religious beliefs are shaped by media polls?

How have I built up my self-worth from my vision of myself as an image of God?

What methods do I use to prevent status and possessions from being the sources of my identity?

How do I resist the negative ideology of the sexual revolution?

What steps have I taken to ensure my confidence that I really can know truth?

What helps me to appreciate the mystery of the human person?

How often do I think of my body as a temple of the Spirit?

Who are the people in my life that awaken in me a sense of spiritual realities?

Plan to Share Your Faith With Others

Am I afraid to share my faith with others? If so, why? What will I do about it?

How could a birth, a death, suffering, a move to a new neighborhood, joining a new parish or reaching a certain birthday be occasions for evangelizing?

If my nature is aggressive, how will I temper it in sharing my faith? If my nature is passive, how will I activate it to be brave enough to share my faith?

What approaches will I use to place the Holy Spirit's power at the center of my evangelizing effort?

With whom do I wish I could share my faith? How will I go about it?

An Offer

Suppose Jesus appeared to you and made the following proposal:

I will give you whatever you want. Think of all the wishes you have ever had. Do you want status, money, recognition, sexual pleasure, unlimited power, good looks, the greatest golf swing, the most powerful tennis serve, membership in the world's most exclusive clubs, the ability to disappear and reappear somewhere else without cars or planes or walking? Everything will be permitted. Consider nothing you want to be a sin. I can make your impossible dreams come true. You will not die. You will live forever. Only one thing I will not give you. You will never meet me or see me or enjoy my company.

What do you think of the proposal?

How did the last line affect you?

What does your response tell you about yourself?

If you accepted Christ's proposal, could you still remain a Christian? Why or why not?

What relationship does your reaction to the proposal have to evangelizing?

Centering Prayer

For centering prayer (see pages 71-73), use this teaching from Paul: "I am not ashamed of the gospel" (Romans 1:16a).

Prayer

Jesus, my evangelizer, you have called me to receive the gift of salvation and the Kingdom. Graciously, you brought me into the Church, met me in your sacraments and enlightened me with your catechesis. Mercifully, you showed me how to be a witness to your desires for the world.

Next, you made it clear that the converted must undertake the ministry of converting others. I, the evangelized, should become an evangelizer. Remind me then to envision each person as a mystery, not a problem to be solved. Show me how to respect the freedom of others even as I offer them your gift which will make them experience greater freedom.

Grant me the courage to share my faith in you. Stir up my imagination to find a thousand ways to speak of your love to others. Never allow me to forget to will the goal you set for me. Then I can find the grace-filled means to achieve it.

Chapter Nine

Jesus, My Cross-Bearer

Four Reasons for the Crucifixion

Of all the Holy Week ceremonies, the one that
touches me most is the adoration of the cross on
Good Friday. While the ritual is basically the same
everywhere, parish churches and monasteries have
developed unique ways to do it. The most moving I
have experienced is at the Norbertine Abbey of
Daylesford in Paoli, Pennsylvania. Norbertine Father
Andrew Ciferni designed this ceremony in
consultation with the Abbey liturgical team.

The austere abbey church provides four areas for
the standing-room-only crowd of worshipers: the
choir, the assembly section and the two arms of the
transept. The people surround a simple stone altar—
no altar coverings, no candles, just a plain, jagged,
consecrated stone which represents Christ.

A period of silence precedes the procession of
the cross. Then a musician plays a tuba solo. The
music is an original composition by Father Mark
Falcone, a funeral march well suited to the haunting
sound of the tuba and the solemn memory of Christ's
Way of the Cross.

A barefoot woman wearing a floor-length white

robe leads the procession. Four young men, also barefoot, white-bloused and blue- jeaned, carry an enormous cross in the horizontal position. There is no corpus on the wood. Instead there is a relic of the true cross embedded in its center. A richly textured red fabric covers the main part of the cross.

The procession slowly circles the altar until it returns to face the nave. The tuba stops. The men lift the cross to a vertical position. As a cantor sings, "This is the wood of the cross...," they unveil a portion. The people in the nave kneel in adoration. The procession moves to the left transept, repeats the ritual, unveiling another part. Then to the choir and finally to the right transept: Now all the worshipers are kneeling in communal adoration.

As they unveil the last section of the cross, they unfurl the red veil over the altar and let it come to rest on the altar table. The covering of the cross has become the altar cloth. The adoration of the cross is integrated with the sacrificial altar of Jesus.

The closing half of the Good Friday liturgy follows immediately. The individual veneration of the cross occurs after the liturgy. Every single one of the hundreds of adults, teenagers and children in attendance come forward for this act of devotion.

I believe the ritual speaks for itself; no extra comment from me is needed. Naturally, its truest impact comes only from the experience. A description cannot replace that. But the scene does set the mood for our reflection on Jesus, my Cross-Bearer.

Why the Cross?

In Chapter Seven, "Jesus, My Savior," I asked the question, "Why the Incarnation?" Why did the Son of God become a human being? I drew my answer from a painful look at human sinfulness and God's love, which responded to that condition by the mystery of Christ's birth at Bethlehem. From the words of Christmas carols and the sermons of the Fathers, I found ways to articulate God's reasons for the Incarnation. Christmas tells us why God gave us a Savior.

Holy Week teaches us why the cross was necessary to accomplish salvation. Jesus journeyed from the wood of the crib to the wood of the cross to complete his saving task. Christmas explains the need for salvation. Holy Week narrates the process by which salvation was achieved. To speak of reasons for the cross is not to deal with human logic. We face here the divine logic of God's heart. Rather than the calculative reason of the human mind, this is the wild abandon of love revealed by a divine heart.

The mystery of the cross is rich in reasons. For our purposes I have selected four which seem the most helpful for our growth in faith. Why the cross?

To Give Meaning to Suffering and Death

"And just as Moses lifted up the serpent in the desert, so must the Son of Man be lifted up, so that everyone who believes in him may have eternal life" (John 3:14). The two worst outcomes of sin are pain and death. Nothing bothers moderns more than the senselessness of suffering. Rabbi Harold Kushner dramatized this in his book, *When Bad Things Happen to Good People*. He and his wife suffered a crisis of meaning when they watched helplessly as their beloved son died of progeria, a disease of premature aging. His book is a confession of pain and puzzlement. He raises an agonizing question, "Why does God let children suffer? Why is there pain and death?"

He shares with us his fatherly courage and paternal warmth. He gives us a thoughtful response to his question: God is all-loving and good, but God is not all-powerful. God cannot touch the world's suffering. It must go its inevitable way. I sympathize with him and admire his honest struggle to find wisdom in his darkness. But I submit that his solution is incomplete.

Jesus gives us the rest of the answer. God is love, but God is also power and can affect the world. Pain and death occur because of sin. "The wages of sin is death" (Romans 6:23a)—spiritual and physical death. I may suffer and die either due to my own sins or because of the general sinfulness. Unless we see the connection we will not understand the cross. (Read Romans 1—6 for a fuller explanation of the link between death and sin.) Jesus said he must be lifted up on the cross so that we might survive our physical death and have eternal life.

Pain and death are more than medical questions. They are spiritual and moral ones. Jesus chose what we hate most (suffering and death) to deliver us from what God hates most (sin). He did not come to take away pain and death from this world, but to use it to open for us the doors of glory to the next world. "Was it not necessary that the Messiah should suffer these things and enter into his glory?" (Luke 24:26).

The Passion is a moral drama. It will never make sense to us unless we believe this. Recall that we are dealing with *faith* reasons. The Passion is a fight between good and evil. The signs and symbols are a betrayal kiss, a cowardly denial, an unjust trial, spit, slaps, beatings, thorns dug into a skull, bleeding, nails, jeers, thirst and pain, pain, pain.

The purpose—that is, the meaning—of all this is to defeat the power of immorality and evil over our lives. Jesus embraced what we all dislike fiercely, pain and death, and made it serve the purpose of delivering us from obsession with evil and its enchantment. He killed off death by removing its dead end, not by eliminating its happening here.

If we do not believe in our immortality and the reality of heaven, we will never understand the cross or the role of suffering and death in our lives. It will never make sense. If we think this earth is the only home we will ever have, then pain and death will always be insane to us. Only when we wake up and realize what our final destiny is—namely, to be with absolute Love for all eternity—will we both see the logic of the cross and kneel in silence and awe before it.

In John's Gospel "lifted up" describes both the lifting up of Jesus to death and his rising up to glory. At the very moment of death the sunrise of life is seen. Just when darkness should have banished light, lightning struck the earth and the possibility of heaven was made available to all. The blood and water that flowed from Christ's side tell us of the birth of the Church and the sacraments that assure us we already begin to experience heavenly life before our physical deaths.

Only the cross gives meaning to suffering and death. When, by faith, we unite our own pain and death to that of Jesus, we share in the victory over sin and evil. No other answer will work. No other solution will satisfy us. We may fight it, rage against it, think it unfair. Only when we accept it in faith will we come to wisdom.

Jesus Walks With Us

Human pain is everywhere. An old man sits home alone the day after his wife dies. A mother hesitates to open the door, fearing the message that her son has died in battle. A father loses his job and wonders how he will support his family. Parents quarrel and frighten their children.

We know the cross as the Passion of Jesus. It is also an act of *compassion* (from the Latin for "to suffer with").

A story in the Book of Daniel foresees this truth (see Daniel 3:1-97). Centuries ago, the Jewish people were deported to Babylon. The cruel king Nebuchadnezzar mounted a statue of himself outside the walls of the city. People were expected to worship the statue as though it were a god. Dissidents were thrown into a furnace.

Three Jewish refugees refused to obey these orders. The guards threw them into the fire. Then an odd thing happened: The Jews walked through the fire unharmed. Not even their hair was singed. But the most amazing thing of all was the sight of a fourth person walking with them. That fourth person was God.

Isaiah wrote of God's compassion for those in pain in words that echo this story:

> When you pass through the water, I will be with you;
>> in the rivers you shall not drown.
> When you walk through fire, you shall not be
>> burned;
>> the flames shall not consume you. (Isaiah 43:2)

God wants to walk with us in our pain. Jesus did this in his ministry by healing hearts, minds and bodies. But he knew that in this life, even if he is with us, we will still have pain. His cross is a message to us that he is willing to share our pain so we will always realize he knows what it is like. He experiences our pain and brings to it the inner peace that is possible despite the suffering. Jesus promises to be our strength and refuge, always present to help us in time of trouble. When we meditate on the cross we sense the credibility of his promise.

During his earthly life Jesus often prayed the psalms—verses such as this:

> Trust in him at all times, O my people!
>> Pour out your hearts before him.
> God is our refuge! (Psalm 62:9)

He lived by that teaching and assured us that he will be the one we can turn to in our suffering: "Come to me, all you who labor and are burdened, and I will give you rest" (Matthew 11:28).

Jesus is as close to us as the prayer we utter, even

closer. He is our constant support. In the solemn glow of the cross, we gain the power to bear our own suffering with courage and hope. If Jesus had never known our pain, we might find it hard to believe that he wants to walk with us. Gazing at his helpless form, we experience his capacity to be our rock and our refuge.

A Criterion for Evaluating the World

Many people live and die without looking deeply at the meaning of the world in which we live. They muddle through life from day to day, taking things as they come. Pleasure and pain guide them. Seldom do reason, principles and conscience control how they think about life. The urge to acquire a coherent view of life does not occur to them.

Many others, however, stimulated by intellectual curiosity and thoughtfulness of mind, look more profoundly at life. They encounter riddles, perplexities, contradictions, enigmas—the mystery of it all. A host of questions clamor for answers. Should I trust in the power of positive thinking? Or ought I see the world as absurd, as the existentialists do? Will it be best to eat, drink and be merry and treat the whole world in a light-hearted manner? Or should I furrow my brow and ponder the seriousness of it all? Would taking refuge in history unlock the secret of life, or would being a futurist be a better posture? These honest searchers strive to harmonize what they see in the world with their inner need to find a key to understanding it and apply it to their behavior.

We are companions with the second group

mentioned above. But our question flows from our faith. We ask, "What is the Christian view of life? What does revelation tell us about how to evaluate the world?" The response of revelation is the cross, the death of the Son of God made flesh. If we place beside the cross all the matters that people think are important, those things are put in perspective.

Bring forward the power people of the world: the men and women in command of nations and the corporate empires; the rock stars and entertainment stars wrapped in stretch limos, furs and jewels; the wealthy who move from one fabulous estate to the other; the chairpersons of the great boardrooms. Notice all the people who serve them, the people who make their beds and cook their food. In imagination, ask them to come, one by one, and stand next to the cross. What do you see in the contrast? What is the worth of it all?

Visualize the nations. Summon the economic and military superpowers. Count the money they spend on weapons and trade wars. See the smaller ones, often riven by the same strife and wars as the big ones. Feel the jealousies and the envy. Experience the intensity and energy that motivates them. Recall the English poet Thomas Gray's words, "The paths of glory lead but to the grave." Situate the powers of the world for a moment at the foot of the cross. What is the worth of it all?

Open the door to the world of science and intellect. Meet the geniuses of satellite technology, the barons of communication, researchers in biochemistry and the cures for AIDS and cancer, the novelists, playwrights and poets, think-tank analysts, counselors to presidents and kings. Invite them, one by one, to stand by the cross. Measure them by that comparison. What think you? What is the worth of it all?

Finally, lift the curtain that tries to hide the poor and the suffering from us. See the homeless, the political prisoners, the street kids of Rio, the crowded families of Calcutta, the black shantytowns in South Africa, the children of war in Belfast and Beirut, refugees everywhere. Go to hospices and experience the last days of the dying. Gently lead them to the space beneath the cross. What is your reaction? What is the worth of it all?

Christian revelation teaches us that all things gravitate to the cross. As Jesus said, "And when I am lifted up from the earth, I will draw everyone to myself" (John 12:32). Many object that this approach is too gloomy. The world is a more cheerful place. We have the capacity for enjoyment, and the world supplies the means to get it. The teaching of the cross gets in the way.

The Adam and Eve story gives the same message. The forbidden tree was good for food, so attractive and desirable, so innocently cheerful. The eating of that food had a sour result. The forbidden tree still exists in our culture. Christianity tests us by telling us that this kind of available pleasure should be resisted—that our happiness depends on resisting it. One of the truly superficial dogmas of our time is the view that life is made for happiness. That is true only in the ultimate sense: We are made for the permanent joy of heaven, not the temporary pleasures of this life. Happiness is eternal joy, not brief

pleasures. Joy arises from spiritual fulfillment.
Cardinal John Henry Newman tells us,

> The world is sweet to the lips, but bitter to the taste.
> It pleases at first, but not at last. It looks gay on the
> outside, but evil and misery lie concealed within....
> Therefore the doctrine of the Cross of Christ does
> but anticipate for us our experience of the world.... If
> we will not acknowledge that this world has been
> made miserable by sin, from the sight of Him on
> whom our sins were laid, we shall experience it to be
> miserable by the recoil of those sins upon ourselves.

On the surface the glittering images of the world
seem relatively harmless. The world looks bright.
The cross appears too repelling. But the world is
surface; the cross is depth. Our first real encounter
with it awakens resistance, even revolt. Peter felt that
when he impulsively and protectively objected to
Christ's words about his cross: "God forbid, Lord! No
such thing shall ever happen to you" (Matthew
16:22b).

The silent principle of the cross is not evident in
the surface life of the world, only in the quiet place of
our hearts. Committed Christians, like St. Paul, "live
by faith in the Son of God who has loved me and given
himself up for me" (Galatians 2:20b). Christians who
live by this rule of the cross appear ordinary and as
contented as one would like to see any man or
woman. They have discovered the heart of religion.

We cannot see a heart, but we know it works to
circulate the blood within. Poets tell us it is the center
of emotion. It is not like our eyes, planted on our face,
seeing all and there for all to see. The heart is hidden,
but nonetheless essential for our lives.

The cross is like our hearts: hidden from view but critical for our evaluation of the world. It should be the control center of our lives. Those who are closest to the cross say little about it. They live it. If impelled to speak of it, they share it with the suffering of the world. They converse about it with those who need a rule of life; they open its mystery to those who have struggled to frame deep questions about life's goals.

The cross is not meant to make us sad. Jesus focused on the joy of Christianity. He said its outcome is like the woman in labor who forgets the pain because she is so overjoyed by the baby who is born. The cross is not opposed to joy. Its wisdom tells us not to begin with pleasure, but to delay gratification so that more lasting joy can be achieved. First the sorrow, then the joy; first Good Friday, then Easter Sunday.

The innocent pleasures of the world are symbols of the eternal happiness that God plans for us. Jesus began Holy Week with a parade. It had all the pleasurable features—excitement, waving palms, exultant songs. Jesus could take no real pleasure in it because it was an empty show. The cheers very soon become jeers. It was unreal. At best it was only a hint, a symbol of what was to come. His genuine triumphal march was the Way of the Cross. He would only enter glory through the suffering of the cross.

The Spiritual Value of Obedience

Paul told the Philippians that the Son of God emptied himself of the status of glory, became human and was obedient unto death, even the death of the cross (see Philippians 2:7-8). If ever there was an unpopular word or value in our culture, it is *obedience.* It sounds so un-American. In a culture where freedom is the most admired value, obedience sounds like a throwback to monarchical times and slave cultures. Let the grovelers obey. We are a free people.

Freedom does deserve our vigilance and active defense. Correctly, we praise the peoples of Eastern Europe for overturning the slave cultures in which they lived for decades. We support organizations for human rights. We praise "freedom fighters" and sing lustily of the "land of the free."

Yet some people in our culture have introduced unwarranted limits to freedom. In the name of cultural correctness, an artist can display a blasphemous image of the crucifix at an exhibit subsidized with public money. But woe to those who protest this. The offended must obey the new canons of correctness. The excesses of political correctness on some college campuses remind us that obedience is hardly dead, just co-opted for purposes that suit a given authority. It is precisely these wrong uses of authority that give obedience a bad name.

No other human has ever given the impression of being more free than Jesus. Yet he was not ashamed to obey. He obeyed his parents. He obeyed the rituals of Jewish religion, except when the rules dehumanized people and missed the purpose of the commands. "The sabbath was made for man, not man for the sabbath" (Mark 2:27b). He obeyed civil laws and paid his taxes (see Matthew 17:24-27).

The greatest test of his obedience was at Gethsemane when he pleaded with his Father to change his mind about the Passion. The beauty of that scene is that it convinces us that obedience was just as hard for Jesus as for us—even more so, for we are rarely asked to obey a call to blood martyrdom.

Obedience of this kind makes sense only when viewed from faith. Such obedience must not be seen purely in terms of slavish submission to an impersonal law. When about to make his most critical act of obedience, Jesus dialogued with his Father. The obedience took place in a profoundly personal encounter.

As is the case with pain and death, obedience must also be viewed in terms of its religious consequences. Clues to this can be found in the human potential movement. Each of us is born with potential. Some say that potential is blocked by inner emotional turmoil caused by internalized taboos. They argue that liberation of our potential comes from revolt against these restrictions. Others claim that it is imprisoned by social circumstances. Liberation of our potential is caused by revolt against repressive social and economic forces.

Psychologist Abraham Maslow taught us that human potential can be unblocked by believing we have a pyramid of needs which, when satisfied in a suitable manner, will result in human fulfillment. There is no need to revolt against legitimate cultural conventions. We have within us the power to grow. We can be inner-directed. Victor Frankl, who survived incarceration in one of Hitler's concentration camps, went further and claimed we have an inborn drive to meaning, even when locked in a death camp.

Jesuit theologian Karl Rahner takes a similar

approach in the realm of spirituality: Each of us is born with the drive to self-transcendence. God has planted this forward-moving energy within us. God is both the source of our inner-directed thrust and also the objective fulfillment of it. Crudely put, God makes us an arrow, acts as archer and serves as the bull's-eye.

Rahner uses the expression *obediential potency* to describe this truth about human nature. We have the potential; to reach perfect fulfillment we must obey the potential within us. Obeying it means letting it soar toward the goal for which it was made. Obedience helps us meet God. Seen in this light, obedience is just what the doctor ordered for our true happiness and fulfillment. Here "doing what comes naturally" means an unimpeded rush toward the highest good, the solution to our desire for happiness.

What stops us? Disobedience—the refusal to obey the movement of our potential toward its instinctive end. Disobedience to the laws of our own nature is the worst kind because it assures us a life of frustration and misery.

The reason we disobey so much external authority is that we already disobey the laws of our inner life. Refusal to obey our proper potential assumes the form of external arrogance, rebelliousness and resistance to legitimate authority. The drama of disobedience begins in our inner life.

Genesis tells us that the first sin was disobedience. Adam and Eve disobeyed their own potential as persons and the God who gave them the gift. The temptation scene deals with changing their inner selves: "[Y]ou will be like gods" (Genesis 3:5b).

The tempter convinced them to disobey the laws of their own humanity and of the God who made them. They sinned internally and expressed it externally by eating the forbidden food.

The New Testament descriptions of salvation connect obedience with Christ's saving act. The grace of Christ's obedience on the cross saved us from the consequences of the disobedience in Eden. The tree of Eden is replaced with the tree of the cross. The possibilities of obedience for fulfillment are restored.

Love and Suffering Together

Toward the end of his life, Francis of Assisi was preparing himself to celebrate the feast of the Exaltation of the Holy Cross (September 14). He asked Brother Leo to open the Gospels three times and give him passages for his meditation. Each time, the book opened to sections from the Passion. Francis took these Scripture verses with him to Mount Alverno.

An angel appeared to him in a dream. He said he would play a melody on his violin while Francis prayed. The angel played only one note. It was so full of love and harmony that it caused Francis to believe he would go straight to heaven if it continued.

At midnight the feast of the Holy Cross began. Francis asked God to let him feel the pain of Jesus in his passion. He also asked to be filled with the love that moved Jesus to take the cross to save sinners. An angel, clothed with fire, came to him. Francis saw Jesus crucified in the center of the fire. The figure of the Crucified touched him. Francis felt the love he had begged for. He saw the wounds of Jesus on his hands, feet and heart. He experienced Christ's agony and ecstasy. He became a living sign of the cross.

Prayer and faith serve us best when we come to the cross. It is an invitation to experience love and suffering simultaneously, like the agony and ecstasy of Francis. Silence makes the best guide. An open heart expresses the best attitude. Jesus will know what to do. All we need to do is to *be*.

Reflection

From St. Paul to Mother Teresa, the cross has provided occasion for the moral and spiritual conversion of millions. The power of the cross both signifies and causes peace of heart for all who are open to its invitation. No act of Jesus more clearly asserts his love than his crucifixion. The noble texts of the Passion narratives in the Gospels were the first message preached by the apostles; they remain the supreme motivators today for profound personal change. The exercises below are paths to the cross and to the life and love found there.

Why Did I Take the Cross?

Reflect on these words from an ancient Holy Saturday homily:

See on my face the spittle I received
  in order to restore to you the life I once breathed
    into you.
See there the marks of the blows I received
  in order to refashion your warped nature into my
    image.
On my back see the marks of the scourging I
    endured
  to remove the burden of sin that weighs on your
    back.
See my hands nailed firmly to a tree,
  for you who once wickedly stretched out your
    hand to a tree.
I slept on the cross and a sword pierced my side
  for you who slept in paradise and brought forth
    Eve from your side. My side has healed the pain
      in yours.

For the next five days, use one of these sayings each day for a moment of prayer at the beginning of each hour you are awake. If your schedule allows it, devote a few minutes at the start of the hour to letting the prayer take hold of you.

Write out the saying that touches you most and put it on your pillow. Go to sleep with that teaching in your mind.

When you have shared prayer with your family or with a group of friends, bring them these five teachings about the passion of Jesus and offer them as prayer starters.

Consciousness Raising

The cross gives meaning to suffering and death.

> How have I come to understand that pain and death are moral and spiritual matters as well as medical ones?

> What is the connection between heaven and the cross?

> How do I cope with my own pain?

Jesus walks with us in our pain.

> What have I learned from the story of the fourth person in the fiery furnace?

> Suppose Jesus had come, been an inspiring teacher, never had any major sickness and died a quiet death. How would he then help me with my suffering?

The cross helps us evaluate the world.

> When I place my attitudes about money, sex and power beneath the cross, what do I see?

> What does it mean to say that the cross should be like my heart, the hidden principle of my life?

> How is it possible that I could bear my cross and still be happy?

The cross teaches the spiritual value of obedience.

> In what ways does obedience make me feel uncomfortable?

> What examples from Christ's life motivate me to obedience to God's will?

> What experiences of my inner life teach me the value of obeying the moral impulses of my soul?

Prayer

In the solemn glow of the cross I kneel to pray:
  Hail blessed wood!

I see my Savior gathering up my sins and obey:
  Praise be to Jesus!

I experience Christ's bringing God and the world into one:
  Glory be to God!

I feel the pull of all creation to this hill:
  Bless you, Lord!

I hear your seven words of submission to God's will:
  May angels adore you!

My sins are washed away by the blood of the Lamb:
  May creation worship you!

My mind has cleared and my heart is full of love:
  May all people love you!

Chapter Ten

JESUS, MY JOY

Experiencing Easter

On Easter 1991 I was in Lvov, Ukraine. I participated in the first Catholic liturgy to be held in St. Yuri's Cathedral in forty-three years. Gorbachev was still ruling in Moscow, but the old order was crumbling. Religious freedom was taking hold. At fifteen minutes before midnight on Holy Saturday, we assembled in the cathedral and lit our candles. Then, according to the Greek Catholic ritual, we left the building and marched in procession around the outside, as though in search of Jesus.

Returning to the door, we stood in the starlight and heard the deacon sing the Easter Gospel. When he came to the words, "Why do you seek the living one among the dead? He is not here, but he has been raised" (Luke 24:5b-6a), Cardinal Lubachivsky chanted, *"Christos Voskrese!* Christ is risen!" We responded, *"Voistinu Voskrese!* He is risen indeed!" The cathedral doors opened and we flowed into the church like a communal river of joy.

It was the first time in my life that I experienced so close a connection between liturgy and history. In the liturgy we celebrated the Resurrection of Jesus. In history we rejoiced at the resurrection of six million Ukrainian Catholics from the tomb of persecution and oppression. The music of faith and grace triumphant surged through the cathedral. We were *alleluias* from head to toe.

Stories of Joy

At Easter Jesus appeared to men and women who had begun to lose hope. He opened their eyes to what the Scriptures had foretold: that first he must die, then rise and ascend to his Father's glorious presence.

> This is the day the LORD has made;
> let us be glad and rejoice in it. (Psalm 118:24)

The Father raised up Jesus, the Lord of life. Now Jesus will raise us up by his power. Jesus shines in our darkness to lead us to life and joy and holiness. St. Paul overflowed with joy in the knowledge that spiritual health was restored to the human race. Death entered the world through Adam, but Jesus has given life back to the world (see Romans 5:12-21).

The Easter Vigil, both in the early Church and today is a joyful celebration of Baptism for new believers. People are born to new faith from the life-giving fountain of the Church. An ancient Easter homily observes, "As they emerge from the grace-giving womb of the font, a blaze of candles burns brightly beneath the tree of faith. The Easter festival brings the grace of holiness from heaven to men [and women].... Fostered at the very heart of holy Church, the community worships the one God, adoring the

triple name of his essential holiness..." (from an
Easter homily by an ancient author, Office of
Readings, Volume II, page 583).

The Gospels are full of Easter stories of joy. Here
I'll explore three: Christ's appearances to Mary
Magdalene, to the Emmaus disciples and to the
eleven apostles. Each narrative unlocks the potential
for joy in our own hearts.

Magdalene

Jesus honored Mary Magdalene with his first
resurrection appearance. He had come to save
sinners and reserved his first Easter appearance for a
woman from whom he had driven seven devils (see
Luke 8:1-3). Just as divine love drove him to appear to
her, so that same love pushed her to look for him.
Magdalene embodied these scriptural sentiments:

> ...I will seek
> Him whom my heart loves....
> The watchmen came upon me,
>   as they made their rounds of the city:
>   Have you seen him whom my heart loves?
> I had hardly left them
>   when I found him whom my heart loves.
> I took hold of him and would not let him go....
> (Song of Songs 3:2c-4c)

She paced the grounds near the empty tomb. She
would not leave it. She looked for the one she had not
found. In her longing for Jesus, she wept, burning
with the fire of love for him. Her two companions left,
but she stayed. Love inspires perseverance. At first
she sought but did not find. Desire grows stronger

with testing; anticipation fires up desire. David understood the kind of desire and longing we see in Magdalene:

> Athirst is my soul for God, the living God.
> When shall I go and behold the face of God?
> (Psalm 42:3)

Then Mary saw a man at the tomb. She did not recognize him. She thought he was a gardener.

The theme of nonrecognition of Jesus is common in the Easter narratives. Why? For three reasons: First, because Christ's followers were not credulously expecting his resurrection. Second, there was something different about Christ's risen body. St. Paul explained this to the Corinthians, "[The body] is sown corruptible; it is raised incorruptible.... It is sown weak; it is raised powerful. It is sown a natural body; it is raised a spiritual body" (1 Corinthians 15:42b-44a). The Christ of Easter is the same as the Jesus of history, but his body is different: incorruptible, powerful, spiritual. A final reason for non-recognition was that faith was required to recognize the real Jesus.

Jesus asked Mary why she wept. She told him she was looking for Jesus. He called her by name: "Mary!" When she heard Jesus call her name, she recognized him. Joyfully she responded in faith by calling him *rabbouni,* "teacher," and kneeling at his feet. Jesus asked her not to hold onto him. He was not against being touched; he would later invite Thomas to touch his wounds. But he said he must go to his Father. His presence in the garden was temporary; his presence in heaven would be permanent.

Besides, she must learn that joy and love are not possessed, but that she would be possessed by them. Joy and love are bigger than we are, too big to hold in our arms. That is why lovers say they are "in" love, for love possesses them, not the other way around. It is the same with joy. Enraptured people feel like jumping, dancing, singing, laughing. They feel overtaken by joy.

Jesus urged her to let go of him and go tell the apostles the Good News. He made her the preacher to the apostolic college. The believers of the Middle Ages loved that scene and named her *apostola apostolorum*, "apostle to the apostles." The joy that possessed her heart surged to her lips.

When Jesus is my joy I will have the same dynamism as Magdalene. I must go through the steps of her experience. I know that Jesus seeks me. I must look for Jesus. The Lord will call me by name. I am expected to respond in faith. The process of seeking, hearing and responding results in meeting Jesus and being possessed by his love and joy.

The Road to Emmaus

The second story of joy occurs on the road to Emmaus on Easter afternoon (see Luke 24:13-35). Two disciples, one named Clopas, sadly journeyed away from the tragedy of Good Friday, hopeless and depressed. Jesus came up to them, again unrecognized, and took them through a seven-step process from despair to joy. First, he urged them to tell him their story; he helped them express the sorrow in their hearts. Next, he encouraged them to ask the questions that were on their minds. He did not immediately try to answer them. It was more important that he draw them out of their tunnel into the light. Articulating their questions was the best way to do that.

Third, he made them into a small friendship group, gave them a sense of community. Then they were ready for a Scripture lesson, for the doctrinal teachings that would illumine their faith. The fifth step is the gift of joy, of the burning heart. They find themselves so possessed by love that they cannot let Jesus go when they arrive at Emmaus, a name that means "warm wells." They find communion with Jesus in the sixth step, the breaking of the bread. Jesus reveals himself to them, then vanishes, just as he visibly left Magdalene. In the seventh stage, they return immediately for the seven-mile walk back to Jerusalem to proclaim the Good News, just as Magdalene did. Possessed by joy, they can do little else but speak about it.

The Apostles

The third story of joy occurred in the Upper Room on Easter night, according to John's account (21:19-23). Full of fear, the Eleven had gone there and locked the door against any enemy. Thomas, however, had left them for some undisclosed mission. Jesus appeared to them and said, "Peace be with you" (John 20:19b). He showed them the wounds in his hands and side. "The disciples rejoiced when they saw the Lord" (20:20b).

Jesus breathed on them and gave them the gift of

the Holy Spirit. He anointed them with the Spirit for their evangelizing mission, which would include bringing to the world Christ's forgiveness of sins to those who would come with converted hearts.

Of Faith and Love

These three narratives of joy in the Easter Gospels have common elements: the night of faith and the day of love. The Gospels tell us to love our way to faith. First comes love, then the faith revelation. Magdalene loved, then she believed. The Emmaus disciples first experienced the burning heart of love, then the revelation at the breaking of the bread. The apostles in the Upper Room felt the gift of love in Christ's peace greeting, for the unity of peace is just like the union of love. Then they came to faith in Jesus.

Love is the light that turns on faith. We are inclined to make faith an intellectual matter, as though we could think ourselves into belief. But we know of many brilliant thinkers who know more about Jesus and Catholic teaching than most Catholics, yet they do not have faith or any desire to join the Church. Scripture teaches us to love ourselves into belief. Love Jesus and you will find him. Love Christ and you will believe in him and who he says he is. Love, and believe. St. Paul's great poem about love (1 Corinthians 13:1-13) teaches this same message. Love is the one permanent action that makes all other deeds worthwhile, even faith and hope. Love alone of all virtues will survive our death.

The result is joy. This joy is different from

passing earthly pleasure because it lasts even when we have pain, suffering and other forms of earthly distress. It is caused by the impact of eternal life on time.

Our Journey to Joy

In his book *Heaven*, Peter Kreeft provides an excellent analysis of joy. He acknowledges his debt for its insights to C.S. Lewis's *Surprised By Joy.* I very much like the images and the process he uses to get at the impact of joy on our lives and will share it with you here.

We develop many models to make our inner life clear to ourselves. In Chapter Three I pointed out that the human spirit is a mystery. You may recall I used there Abbot Keating's image of a river to describe the layers of depth we have inside us. In Chapter Five I used three circles to outline the process of losing our ego, losing our "I," and inviting Jesus to be the driving force of our lives. These models are not exact descriptions of our souls. They are hints of the wondrous possibilities we carry within us.

So, let us try another model to address the question of joy. Imagine yourself as a canyon. At the top you stand at the path that enters its depth. Label that your *body.* Midway down the canyon, post another sign saying *soul.* At its bottom erect a marker saying *spirit.* Then we will descend into the canyon, using these markers as steps to permanent satisfaction.

Step One: The Body Seeks Pleasure

Our bodies are the most evident part of ourselves. A body senses. A body sees, hears, tastes, touches and smells. When the senses are pleased, the body feels pleasure. The eye sees a sunrise. The ear hears a melody. The sense of taste awakens to hot chocolate on a cold night. The sense of touch loves an affectionate hug. The smell lingers when bread is baking. The process is body-sensation-pleasure.

But the senses numb. Body pleasure does not last; it is temporary. Moreover, the same process that leads to pleasure also leads to pain.

Step Two: The Soul Seeks Happiness

Step down to the middle of the canyon, the soul within you. This is the home of your mind and your will. The mind knows and the will loves. If the mind obeys its inner nature, it will look for truth. If the will obeys its inner laws, it will choose only goodness. When the mind discovers truth and holds onto it, you will experience happiness. When the will achieves goodness and stays with it, you will experience happiness. This happiness is far more permanent than the pleasures of the body.

Unfortunately, the happiness of a mind enjoying truth and a will resting in the good has its ups and downs. It can be lost, regained and lost again. This is because, like a real canyon, there are storms, counterforces within us that persuade the mind that there is no truth and urge the will to choose evil instead of goodness. Saint Paul described this inner psychology very well:

> ...I know that good does not dwell in me, that is, in
> my flesh. The willing is ready at hand, but doing the
> good is not.... I see in my members another principle
> at war with the law of my mind, taking me captive to
> the law of sin that dwells in my members. For I do
> not do the good I want, but I do the evil I do not
> want. Miserable one that I am! Who will deliver me
> from this mortal body? Thanks be to God [it
> happens] through Jesus Christ our Lord. (Romans
> 7:18-19, 23- 25a)

Because of this inner warfare at mid-canyon level, our
possibilities for lasting happiness are interrupted.

Step Three: The Spirit Seeks Joy

What is the solution? Go deeper. Go to the
bottom of the canyon, to the deepest part of your
inner life, your spirit. That is the stillpoint, the section
of your inner world where Jesus waits to change you
and give you joy and wisdom. That is the meeting
ground between the human being and Jesus. That is
where you learn to find heaven on earth. Better said,
that is where heaven finds you. When you have been
brave enough to make a descent that far, you will rise
in your own Easter with Jesus. You will experience
Jesus, my joy.

The Father has sent us the Holy Spirit to make
this possible. Jesus prayed that this might happen:
"And I will ask the Father, and he will give you
another Advocate to be with you always, the Spirit of
truth" (John 14:16-17a). When our spirit is in touch
with the Spirit on the holy ground at the base camp of

our canyon, we will experience the effects of the Spirit's presence: "love, joy, peace, patience, kindness, generosity, faithfulness, gentleness, self-control" (Galatians 5:22b-23a). The risen Jesus produces a personal Pentecost for us.

Then you realize that joy is a gift. So is wisdom. Joy enchants the will to seek the highest good. Wisdom leads the mind to be possessed by truth. Joy fixes the will in love. You discover that joy and love are greater than yourself. As I mentioned earlier, you will be "in" love. In the chapter, "The End of the Quest: The Joy of Heaven," Kreeft says:

> When joy comes, it indeed "breaks our heart," our containing vessel. For like love, joy is a universal solvent; it cannot be contained. Just as love is not in us, we are "in love" ("It's bigger than both of us"), joy is not in us, but we are in it. "Enter into the joy of your Lord" (Matthew 25:21).

I realize that the words *pleasure, happiness* and *joy* are often used interchangeably, and I will not dispute this usage. One thing is clear: They all denote something we desire—bodily pleasure, soul-filled happiness resulting from knowledge of truth and the will to goodness, spiritual joy. It is also true that our desire wants the absolute, a fulfillment that never fails.

By marking out three steps toward this goal and noting a progress from pleasure to happiness to joy in relation to body, soul and spirit, we gain a useful model for satisfying what our desire pushes us toward. Always remember, this is only one model imposed upon the mystery that is ourselves. The model is not absolute, but the thirst for permanent joy is. Absolute desire wants nothing less than absolute fulfillment. This is one way of seeing how that can happen.

I must say here that the simplicity of the model should not fool us into thinking the steps are easy. The journey to joy is a voyage of challenges, frustrations and sufferings. The simplicity of the image may hide the complexity of the achievement. The walk into the canyon, just like an exploration of a real canyon, is fraught with dangers, detours, darkness, missed directions and storms. Just remember that Christianity makes the best anthropology. It is reality. It includes good and bad, pleasure and pain. It also supplies hope and lasting joy, which anthropology tells us we want so much.

The Feel of Joy

My body can produce pleasure. My soul can create happiness. Only God can make joy. Only God could make anything as astonishing as Easter. If I become an alleluia from head to toe, it is the work of the Holy Spirit in communion with my spirit. What happens to me when I receive the gift of joy?

Joy Is Everlasting

My first experience of joy is its eternal and lasting quality. My pleasures evaporate. My happiness vanishes. Here I encounter a joy that is everlasting. What I produce cannot last. The joy that is from God is eternal. I have said that we journey to a joy that lasts. Objective joy is without end.

Subjectively, I may only experience it intermittently. That is why I must caution you that we may not stay in touch with joy even after we are discovered by it.

We are changeable by nature. We discover Jesus and then we lose him. We find him and forget him. Saints tell us of their battle to remain humbly near Jesus. Yet many saints and millions of good people *do* eventually surrender to Jesus and are governed by joy even in the midst of suffering.

In other words, early encounters with joy are not the end of our spiritual story. They are the beginning. As the Irish say, they are "a little bit of heaven." The taste of joy makes us return to the well. Eventually, God willing, we never stop drinking from the waters of joy. The joy feels new because we never felt it before. It seems old because we know it existed before time. It feels late because we lived so long before finding it. Why else did Augustine say, "Too late have I loved thee, O Beauty, so ancient and so new!"?

Joy Diffuses Itself

The gift of joy is not a private possession. It owns us. We do not own it. The living waters of the well of God demand outlets. Otherwise we would be dead in the water. Go with the flow of joy—up to God with songs of praise and thanks, out to people with the refreshment of hope, into your souls and body with its ecstasy. Joy is irrepressible. If we are in joy, God, the world and self will know it. We do not make a decision to share joy. It makes the decision for us. We minister the flow of joy with the ease of an athlete.

Physical energy naturally diffuses itself. So also does the spiritual energy we call joy. A volcano erupts because of physical necessity. Joy explodes, too—not because of blind necessity, but because of the overflowing love of God. I am not a slave to joy's outbursts. I am like an eagle soaring in its freedom. I do not feel forced to share joy. I am contentedly swept along by its abundant kindness. When I am in its flow, I stand outside myself. That is what the word *ecstasy* (*ek-stasis*) means. Joy diffuses itself.

Joy Is Heavenly

Joy is what God "feels" all the time. It is the permanent condition of heaven. Its diffusion among the Persons in the Trinity is infinite outburst—not by necessity, for nothing forces God, but by sheer abundance. It was this same expansiveness of joy that flowed from the Trinity into the work of creation. The opposite of joy in the next life is hell. Scripture says that hell is eternal death. Hell is the absence of God and the joy intrinsically connected with God. That is why all efforts to describe hell fail. How do you picture an absence? How do you outline the absolute absence of joy?

Jesus used images that give hints of heaven and hell. He said that heaven is like a lot of things: wedding parties, seeds that grow into great trees, leaven that swells a mass of dough. He used only one image for hell: fire. Fire feeds on oxygen. It lives by something else and consumes life.

These images are not exact descriptions, but comparisons that take what we know to help us grasp what we do not know. Those who experience the flood of joy in this life already have a foretaste of heaven. Those who have never known joy can tell us of hell on earth—and hereafter. Hell is the final absence of joy. Heaven is the ultimate and everlasting presence of joy.

Joy Bursts With Praise

Joy causes us to praise God. The geyser of *alleluias* in our Easter liturgy testifies to that. The word *alleluia* comes from the Hebrew and simply means, "Praise Yahweh! Praise God!" Listen to the antiphons for Easter Morning Prayer.

> The splendor of Christ risen from the dead has shone on the people redeemed by his blood, alleluia.
> Our Redeemer has risen from the tomb; let us sing a hymn of praise to the Lord our God, alleluia.
> Alleluia, the Lord is risen as he promised, alleluia.

The praise spoken of here is qualitatively different from the commercial praise in ads or the orchestrated praise of politics. When I read ads for movies, I am struck by the multitude of adjectives: Stunning! Mesmerizing! Spellbinding! An Event! Stupendous! Electrifying! Sportswriters and political public relations people also have a reserve of praise words. We are all weathered enough to know that most of this is "hype" (from *hyperbole*, "exaggeration").

The glut of praise words reminds us that we like to have someone or something extraordinary to praise. It is an altogether human longing. But in a secularized society, we are a bit sheepish about a burst of praise words for God. The one group among us that runs counter to the tide are the Protestant and Catholic evangelicals. They make a loud noise to the Lord and testify that joy has moved them to do so. Modern sensibility—read secularized people, or believers intimidated by them—feels uncomfortable with this.

I do not quibble with style. If a person has experienced the joy of Jesus and wants to shout an *alleluia,* fine. If that person prefers to chant it in the stately Gregorian tones of the Liturgy of the Hours, excellent. If it will be done in humble hymns in a village church eucharistic celebration, superb. If it happens in a deep, silent breath of a prayerful person, terrific. The point is that praising God is good for us because the joy that generates it is so beneficial. People touched by joy need no lessons in praise. They will express it according to their own personality and situation.

Mother of God, Woman of Joy

Mary, the mother of God, is an excellent example of a joyful woman. Strangely, the New Testament does not describe her joy at the resurrection of her son or record Christ's appearance to her. I do not know why, nor will I speculate. There is sufficient evidence of the joy that took possession of her after the conception of Jesus and in her visit to her cousin Elizabeth.

After the Annunciation, Mary journeyed five days to Ain Karim to minister to her cousin, Elizabeth, now in the sixth month of her pregnancy. When Elizabeth heard the sound of Mary's greeting, her child "leaped" in her womb. People consumed with joy are swept off their feet. The old saying is true: "I could have leaped with joy." Heavenly joy urges a person to jump off the earth. Thomas Merton turned that moment into poetry:

> And the unborn saint John
> Wakes in his mother's body,
> Bounds with the echoes of discovery.
> Sing in your cell, small anchorite!
> ...What secret syllable
> Woke your young faith to the mad truth
> That an unborn baby could be washed in the Spirit
>   of God?
> Oh burning joy! ("The Quickening of John the
> Baptist," from *The Tears of the Blind Lions,* New
> Directions)

Mary's visit to her cousin was a Pentecostal event: Elizabeth was "filled with the Holy Spirit" (Luke 1:41b). The physical body of Jesus inside Mary caused an experience of the Spirit, just as, at Pentecost, the Mystical Body of Christ was filled with the Holy Spirit. And Mary was present at that first ecstatic, joyful experience of the Spirit. She brings Jesus, the cause of our joy.

Elizabeth replied with words that would become part of the Hail Mary: "Most blessed are you among women, and blessed is the fruit of your womb" (Luke 1:42b). Clearly, heaven is all mixed up with earth here and joy is the outcome. Mary responded with a song of joy, the Magnificat, which she could just as easily sing again at Easter and Pentecost. She did at that moment what all of Israel's great women had done when filled with God's joy. Miriam took a tambourine in her hand and exploded with a joyful song to celebrate the victory of the Red Sea (Exodus 15:20-21). Hannah, the mother of Samuel, sang about his birth with joyful abandon at the door of the tabernacle of Shiloh (1 Samuel 2:1-10).

Mary poured out the music of the Magnificat. Elizabeth had praised her for her faith; Mary turned the compliment into a chance to praise God. She assimilated praise as a mirror reflects light. She sent it immediately on to God. All the words she sang can be summarized as a grateful, "Thank you, God."

All her words flow from Jesus, her joy. He is the sun; she is the moon. She had let go of her ego and even her "I" so that she could be filled with Jesus. There is no limit to God's yearning to possess us. We are the only ones who can impose a boundary and warn God to come no further. The more we empty our inner life of the possessiveness of the ego and the "I," the more Jesus can fill us with his presence and joy. That is the lesson Mary learned and the one she is only too willing to teach us. The old-fashioned yet ever relevant word for this is *humility*. That is why Mary sang,

> For he has looked upon his handmaid's lowliness;
>   behold, from now on will all ages call me blessed.
> (Luke 1:48)

The mother of God is also the mother of joy.

Believing in Joy

Jesus carried his cross so that we would learn how to carry ours. At Easter he became a sheer effusion of joy to prove to us that our absolute desire for absolute fulfillment is not a myth. What we most deeply want is available to us. The ancient Greeks felt the absolute desire, but concluded it was a useless passion. Their story of Sisyphus, pushing a boulder up a hill and being kicked to the bottom again time after time, evidenced their belief in ultimate frustration. Because we believe in the resurrection of Jesus, we affirm the hope of resurrection—of ultimate joy—for ourselves.

Reflection

Here are some exercises to deepen your hope for a personal Easter and its gift of joy.

Happy Days Can Be Here Again

Think of the canyon model of body-pleasure, soul-happiness and spirit-joy.

To these examples of each, add three from your own experiences:

Body-Pleasure	Soul-Happiness	Spirit-Joy
A satisfying meal	Solved a problem	Sin forgiven
A hug	Helped homeless	Met Jesus
A good song	Visited sick	Gift of prayer

What are examples from your life where body pleasure does not last?

Name three soul-happiness experiences which come and go for you.

List two spirit-joy experiences from your own life, and

one from someone else's.

What does this exercise motivate you to do?

Grief Turned to Joy

Even though it is hard to face the reality of tragedy, it is easy to expect sadness and pain. We fight against pain by seeking pleasure for the body. We run away from sadness by focusing our minds and wills on what we think makes them happy. Because we practice massive denial of tragedy, we fail to seek joy, the gift that sees us through tragedy. We compromise. We try to reduce our pain and sadness with energetic pleasure and happiness substitutes. We let a curtain hide tragedy, but it also conceals joy. If we live like this, then the grief of tragedy never becomes the ecstasy of joy.

Am I ready for joy? Or am I afraid of it?

Using the image of the canyon, am I fixated at the body-pleasure level?

Have I stopped midway at the soul-happiness level?

What must I do to go deeper into my base camp, my spirit-joy level?

Journey to Joy

Jesus took the Emmaus disciples through seven steps to joy: story, tradition, mission, questions, burning hearts, community and celebration.

How many of these seven moments have you known?

Have you had an experience in which you went through all the steps? If yes, relive it.

Which steps have you never known? Why is this so?

Think of three joy-filled people that you know personally or have learned about from reading or from the testimony of others. What is the secret of their joy? Which steps from the Emmaus process do you notice in them? How does this affect your life and resolve?

Prayer

Jesus, my joy, you have risen from the dead to make possible my own resurrection. At the first Easter you immediately brought joy to Mary Magdalene, the Emmaus disciples and the apostles in the Upper Room. Their love for you led them to believe in you. Their faith opened them to the mystery and reality of your resurrection.

Be my love, that I may believe in you. Be my love, that I may hope in you. Be my love, that I may share your joy.

I have often been persuaded to settle for less in life. I allow my body to insist on its pleasure at the expense of my deeper desires. My mind busies itself to the point where it forgets you. My will chooses the good but not the best. Fire up my desire and my longing to live at the deepest level of life, my spirit.

My absolute desire will never be satisfied with anyone but you who are the living Absolute. You are the cause of my joy. I love you. Make me an alleluia from head to toe.

Conclusion

Here we finish our walk through the Christ gallery. We have reflected on ten images of Jesus: friend, healer, teacher, Lord, mentor, servant leader, Savior, evangelizer, cross-bearer, joy. We have barely dipped into these wells of inspiration and joy. Each image is a source for boundless reflection. Each one calls us to personal transformation and a promise of splendid joy. Treat the end of this book as a beginning of your lifelong contemplation of Jesus. Catch his fire. Feel his love. Touch his truth. Burn with his concern for others. Carry the cross with him. Rise with him to a joy that will possess you. Prepare to experience a little bit of heaven on earth.